# Arctic Argonauts

Walter Kenyon

# Arctic Argonauts

Edited for the Press by M. T. Kelly

Picture Editor, Robert Stacey

# Arctic Argonauts

Walter Kenyon

Published by Penumbra Press
Waterloo, Ontario, Canada.

Published with assistance from the block grant programs of the Canada Council and the Ontario Arts Council, for which the publisher and editors express their thanks and appreciation. The Editors also wish to thank Peta Daniels, Department of New World Archeology, Royal Ontario Museum, for assistance with the captions.

ISBN 0 921254 18 0
PENUMBRA PRESS

## Note on the Illustrations

The illustrations in this book were selected from photographs compiled by Dr. Walter Kenyon for reproduction in the two projected volumes of *Arctic Argonauts,* and are reprinted with permission from the Royal Ontario Museum. Sources and locations of original images, where known, are indicated in the captions.

**Front cover**: Mariner's astrolabe, inscribed '1628,' recovered from a wreck at Isle aux Morts, Newfoundland. The astrolabe was a 16th- and 17th-century European navigational instrument used for determining latitude. The user suspended the astrolabe by its ring, and sighted along the moveable sighting-rule (or *alidade*), until the sun, or sometimes the pole star, was aligned through the holes of both the upper and the lower sighting-vanes (or *pinnules*). The angle of the sun, or the star, above the horizon, or below the zenith, was read from the astrolabe scale, and the latitude was calculated from tables. Astrolabes were made heavy, and were often bottom-weighted, to help keep them from swinging back and forth when used onboard a rolling ship. A small amount of movement was inevitable, however, and navigational errors of up to 400 miles were not uncommon. Courtesy, Newfoundland Museum, St. John's.

**Frontispiece & Page 14**: Photographs of Dr. Walter Kenyon (1917-1986). Courtesy, Mrs. Eva Kenyon.

**Back cover:** Cartouche from a *Map of the North Pole and Parts Adjoining,* by M. Pitt, Engraving, with watercolour, from *The English Atlas* (Oxford, 1680). Courtesy, Royal Ontario Museum, Canadian Decorative Arts Department, Toronto (acc. n. 958.36.2).

## Contents

## Introduction

WRITING ABOUT THE GRIMSBY SITE, a historic cemetery, Walter Kenyon concluded that the patterning in death he had been examining so scrupulously and scientifically was 'the final act in the most awful of the rites of passage—a symbolic bridge arching across the dark and terrifying abysses of eternity.' This passage, these large concerns, were typical of Walter Kenyon both as an archaeologist and writer, and as a man. He did hot just see assembled bones, shards of pottery or 'projectile points,' though he listed and catalogued them professionally; always in his work, in his asides and conclusions, is the feeling that what he examined was once held by living human beings.

This is not the approach taken by all archaeologists. In its efforts to be scientific, archaeology, like many human sciences, and especially archaeological writing, can seem barren and disconnected. The geneticist, environmentalist, scientist and broadcaster, David Suzuki, has pointed out that science can be as ruthlessly political and mean-spirted as any human activity, perhaps more so because of claims to purity or objectivity. What distinguishes Kenyon's work, in the posthumous *Arctic Argonauts,* as well as in occasional papers and monographs, is its humanity. His asides, his putting objects and people in context, the intrusion of his personal style, are delightful.

Kenyon begins *Arctic Argonauts* in typical fashion, bluntly pointing out that he is trying to rescue men like Frobisher and Baffin and Jens Munk from obscurity. He says they have been treated 'in much the same way that the Indians and Eskimos are dealt with in most histories of Canada. We nod politely in their general direction, then turn to what we consider to be the more serious business of politics.'

This view of native people is certainly changing, thanks to their own political action and writers and the work of intellectuals such as Bruce Trigger, Ramsay Cook, Jennifer Brown, Sylvie Van Kirk and many others. But Kenyon was never guilty of nodding politely at native people, even though at one point in his career he was arrested for disturbing an Indian burial ground, the very Grimsby site referred to earlier. Kenyon deals with his experience of 'political archaeology' in a paper published by the Royal Ontario Museum titled *Some Bones of Contention.* What is clear from Kenyon's writing is a deep respect for those who had been alive in the past, whom he wanted to know and understand. In the end he said that he had seen enough of bones and graveyards, and perhaps of politics. He wanted his ashes spread over James Bay. There he could be part of that immense northern sky that has looked down on so many living beings for so many thousands of years.

Kenyon intended to structure *Arctic Argonauts* in three phases. He died after completing Phase I and the 'Interlude' (here entitled 'Aftermath') leading up to Phase II, but there is a strange irony here, one Kenyon would have appreciated. He was sensitive to language, and the language of the arctic reports sent to the British Admiralty in the nineteenth century did not lift his heart, though they are a superb record. After dutifully giving the historical background of this period—this was an England caught up in the scientific and industrial revolutions that were reshaping the world—Kenyon gets around to what bothers him: 'Education at the time was structured around a study of the classics. This resulted in a prose style that was lucid, but extremely formal. The spontaneity of the Elizabethans had disappeared, to be replaced in the nineteenth-century journals by an impersonal prose that was clearly derived from the Latin. Its sentences marched across the a Roman legion. The result, in my opinion, is quite depressing.... And furthermore, a prolonged immersion in the self-consciously formal prose of the nineteenth-century journals tends to infect the prose style of the historian himself.'

It didn't happen to Kenyon's prose. He could certainly be idiosyncratic—there is one remark about leaving one of his female archaeological assistants, in a tent on an island in the Arctic, to her 'maidenly sleep'—but his aim was always to make the period he was writing about come alive.

There were paradoxes in his discipline, yet he allowed his personality to come through; he was trained the western scientific tradition, but allowed for other ways of thinking. An extreme example of a discipline or of a cultural bias distorting perception is that of the scientist who sees a singing bird *only* as defending its territory; joy in life from another creature is discounted; a carolling robin is reduced to a miniature developer defending private property. Today, with its emphasis on economics, there is a tendency among some ethnologists and historians to see native people as 'capitalists with feathers.' This is a complex debate, and *Arctic Argonauts* is clear about the economic drive into the Arctic—but Kenyon is direct about how he saw native motives. In *The History of James Bay, 1616-1686,* he writes: 'The Indians, after dealing with the company for some thirty-five years, still operated within a system of interpersonal relationships. Trading, then, was not "shopping" in the modern sense of that peculiar word, for the motivation of the Indian was different from that of the European.'

Kenyon's own motives were complex. Although he was a specialist in the past, he did not like to talk about his own. Born in 1917, one of seven children, he experienced a desperate childhood; perhaps it was the emotional storm that made him an artist. He left home at '13 or 14' to' ride the rails,' and when he married in 1947, his wife Eva had a masters degree and Walter had a grade eight education. He went from marriage to high school to fatherhood; after starting high school at age thirty he continued straight through to the University of British Columbia for his BA and returned to Toronto for his MA. When Kenyon received his PhD in 1951 he was one of the oldest people at that time ever to have a doctorate conferred by the University of Toronto, and his doctorate was in *Canadian* archaeology. Kenyon started at the Royal Ontario Museum in 1956 and while he was there his work, along with that of his late colleague, the ethnologist Ed Rogers, gave a deserving dignity to Canada's native peoples and the country's ancient past.

Kenyon worked hard. He wrote books and monographs, he dug and catalogued and edited, and he smoked cigars. It is significant that even those of his peers who sometimes disagreed with him, such as archaeologist C.S. 'Paddy' Reid, thought of Kenyon with affection. Reid is a passionate and energetic man; he does not think southern archaeology had paid enough attention to the north. There is a similarity to Kenyon in that, introducing *Boreal Forest and Sub-Arctic*

*Archaeology* (London Chapter, Ontario Archaeological Society, 1988), Reid is not afraid to mention his own 'brush with death.' His testimony is eloquent: 'Go anywhere along Rainy River and mention Walter and people still talk of him as if he was a legend. Hell, he is a legend with people along the river.' Out of this legendary sojourn came one of Kenyon's last books, *Mounds of Sacred Earth*. It is true he is remembered. Chief Willie Wilson of the Manitou Rapids Reserve, who plans a memorial to the great mounds, only met Kenyon once but sensed that Walter, although alien and looking at the Long Sault Rapids from another perspective, also felt the place was 'sacred, central.'

I never met Walter Kenyon when he was alive; I don't know how he looked, or walked, or his peculiar way of talking. I can get a picture through the memory of his friends and family, and above all his books. But there is something more. Like Frobisher and Munk and Baffin, whom Kenyon tries to bring to live in the following pages, but also like Matonabee and David Thompson and Crowfoot, Kenyon, because of his passionate commitment, has become part of the 'symbolic bridge' he wrote about. Symbols have power. Those who walked the earth Walter Kenyon dug into can be referred to in the covenant chain of the Iroquoians, the spirits of the Algonquians, or the great chain of being of western thought. Something remains, something is alive, if those of us still here will listen: 'part of the land, part of the water.'

— M. T. Kelly

# Preface

TO WRITE YET ANOTHER BOOK on the search for a northwest passage might appear to be a redundancy. There are, after all, endless volumes already devoted to that topic, and many of them are surprisingly good. On the other hand, many, and perhaps the majority of existing works, are concerned primarily with the hapless Franklin expedition and with the many search-parties that were sent to find him. In these volumes, such early explorers as Frobisher and Baffin are relegated to a slender introductory chapter. They are treated in much the same way that the Indians and Eskimos are dealt with in most histories of Canada: we nod politely in their general direction, then turn to what we consider to be the more serious business of politics.

If we actually pause to look at those early explorers, however, we find a list of thirteen men whose names are—or should be—household words in Canada. With one exception, they were all Englishmen, and they had all been sent in search of the passage by merchants, not politicians. That is, the initial probe of our arctic waters, from 1576 to 1632, had nothing whatever to do with colonial expansion or visions of empire; nor was it concerned at all with the spread of Christianity. It was a purely commercial enterprise. The single exception was Jens Munk, a native of what is now Norway, who was sent to seek out a passage by Christian IV of Denmark, who ruled over both countries at the time. Munk added nothing to our knowledge of arctic geography but did leave us a vivid description of his expedition of 1619-20, and of his wintering at the mouth of the Churchill River in what is now the province of Manitoba. Munk's journal, by the way, is the earliest surviving record of a wintering in arctic Canada.

This initial or commercial phase of the story began in 1576 with the first voyage of Martin Frobisher. It ended seventy-six years later, in 1632, when Thomas James returned from wintering on Charlton Island in James Bay. He reported to the merchants who had funded the expedition that Hudson and James Bay had now been thoroughly explored, and that there was no northwest passage. He conceded that such a passage might actually exist, but if it did exist, he pointed out, it must lie in such high northern latitudes that it would have no commercial value. The merchants wisely accepted James' decision, and turned their attentions elsewhere. The search for a northwest passage was abandoned.

After a lapse of 185 years, the second phase of arctic exploration began in 1818. During the intervening period, the western world had changed in some very fundamental ways. The enlightenment of the seventeenth century had jolted humanity out of the accustomed grooves that had shaped existence for millennia. Reason and humanism focused attention on this world rather than the next. The spirit of the age was best symbolized by the study of physical science. It was members of that society who coached the new breed of arctic explorers. For the men of this, the second phase of arctic exploration, were working in the interests of science rather that mammon, although that still fashionable deity was sometimes lurking in the background.

This second phase was almost entirely a naval project. At the end of the Napoleonic wars, Britain was left with the vast fleet she had used to blockade Europe during the hostilities. The Secretary of the Admiralty at the time, John Barrow, was an avid student of geography, and was active in both the Royal Society and the Royal Geographic Society, which he founded. It was relatively simple, therefore, for him to divert a few naval vessels to arctic exploration. In 1818, he dispatched two such expeditions to the north. One, led by Captain David Buchan, was to proceed due north between Spitzbergen and Greenland. The other, led by Captain John Ross, was to sail north up Davis Strait. If they were successful in reaching what was commonly believed to be an open polar sea lying north of the broad fringe of ice, they were to sail to the westward, and exit through Behring Strait.

Barrow's reasoning was plainly and logically set forth:

> The simple fact of a perpetual current setting from the Pacific into Behring Strait, and perpetual current down the coasts of Greenland and Labrador into the Atlantic, renders such a communication extremely probable: and it becomes almost certain when we find the productions of the shores of the Pacific carried to the northward by the first current, and brought down into the

Atlantic by the second (1818, p. 377).

Barrow's purpose then, was to gather geographical and other scientific knowledge of the Arctic. If the expedition were successful, they would, in fact, have sailed through the northwest passage. But the sailing and attendant exploration was now an end in itself. The Arctic was no longer seen as a carrier that had to be overcome in order to reach some distant goal. It was seen, rather, as just another part of an expanding world. And as such, it was just as intriguing to the scientists of England as were the jungles of Africa or the palm-fringed islands of the Pacific.

John Barrow, chief architect of the second phase of explorations, described the Buchan and Ross expeditions as 'the most liberal and disinterested that was ever undertaken, and every way worthy of a great, a prosperous and an enlightened nation: having for its primary object that of the advancement of science, for its own sake, without any selfish or interested views' (1818, p. 379). It was a bold and concerted effort that he launched into the northern mists, and it was successful. In the forty-seven year period between the battle of Waterloo and the outbreak of the Crimean war, the exploration of arctic Canada was virtually completed.

With the geographical problems solved, and with England's energies focused on the Crimea, the Arctic was again left to its timeless fate. It was not until the end of the last great war that our attentions were again drawn northward, thus ushering in the third or current phase of arctic exploration. Fundamentally, this phase has much in common with the first, for they were both commercial ventures. Oil and natural gas have replaced gold and spices as the major economic attractions; powerful steel ships have replaced the frail wooden vessels of Frobisher and Davis. The ice and fog, however, remain the same. The ice that destroyed one of Frobisher's ships, the *Dennis*, off Resolution Island in 1578 is still a threat to any vessel that dares to shoulder its way into the arctic pack. But the lure of riches has that same attraction for the modern investor that it had for the Elizabethan merchant. Martin Frobisher, in all probability, would have felt hopelessly out of place among the explorers of Victorian England, or the learned members of the Royal Society. But he would feel quite at home on a drilling rig on the Beaufort Sea. Profits and glory he could understand.

This entire three act drama is set forth in the following pages.[1] At one level, it is a simple story dealing with navigation, naval architecture, clothing, diet, methods of land transportation, the relationships of the explorers with the Eskimo, and similar topics. On the other hand, it is a complex narrative because of the number of people and expeditions involved, as well as the vast geographical stage on which the drama was played out. The length of the northwest passage would vary with the route taken, and that, in turn, would depend on ice conditions, which change dramatically from one year to the next. In round figures, however, we are talking about a twenty-five hundred mile passage through ice-blocked channels that were liberally strewn with reefs. To chart that vast expanse of ice and rocks was a hurculean task. It was carried out by ships, small boats, dog-teams, canoes and man-hauled sledges. Some idea as to the size of the operation can be gained from the following figures. During Phase I, between 1576 and 1632, four parties wintered in the north, two in James Bay and two in Hudson Bay. During Phase II, between 1819 and 1858, thirty two different arctic expeditions wintered in the north. Because some of them spent more than a single winter there, the total number of winterings adds up to thirty eight. Only twenty eight different sites were used as wintering-places, however, because some of them were used more that once. Throughout the search for the northwest passage, some three hundred men lost their lives, and fifteen ships were either lost or abandoned in the ice.

BY THE MIDDLE OF THE SIXTEENTH CENTURY, both Spain and Portugal were rapidly expanding their overseas trade. Streams of gold and silver were flowing from the Americas to Spain, while argosies of

---

[1] Since Kenyon died while halfway through the writing of the second phase, the present volume includes only the first act and part of the rising action in the intervening years between 1632 and 1818. ED.

East Indian spices were piling up in the warehouses of Portugal. England, meanwhile, had been denied access to the wealth of the newly discovered lands by Papal decree. Sixtus IV had issued a Papal bill in 1481 giving all of West Africa south of the Canary Islands to Portugal. Twelve years later, Pope Alexander IV confirmed Spain's exclusive rights to the New World. But neither Henry VIII of England nor his daughter, Elizabeth, would recognize the right of the popes to apportion the world in such an arbitrary manner. To challenge the authority of Rome by ignoring the papal decrees, however, was obviously unwise because such an act would lead directly to war with Spain. And Spain was in a position to back up her theological arguments with a formidable array of sea-power. If Spain and Portugal could not be too openly challenged, they could perhaps be out-maneuvered by a diplomatic stance that preserved the amenities, but still permitted the English merchants to indulge in some very profitable piracy.

William Hawkins, for example, fitted out the *Paul of Plymouth* at his own expense, and made three long and remarkable voyages to West Africa and Brazil between 1528 and 1530. Technically, he was encroaching on Portuguese territory because of the papal edict of 1481. In this connection, however, matters of conscience as well as matters of state could be dealt with by reference to a prevailing sentiment of the age. For it was widely accepted at the time that an explorer was free to occupy any newly discovered land that was not already occupied by some Christian prince. And Portugal, it was argued, had not really occupied either West Africa or Brazil, but only small parts of them. England's position was expressed most eloquently, perhaps, by Richard Eden (1555). He pointed out that the English merchants could legitimately refuse to have their movements restricted by the arrogance of the Portuguese who, through 'the conquering of fortie of fiftie miles here and there, and erecting of certain fortresses, think to be Lordes of halfe the world, envying that other(s) should enjoy the commodities, which they themselves cannot wholly possesse.'

English overseas expansion entered a period of rapid expansion in 1533 with the Wyndham-Pinteado expedition to Guinea. Organized by a group of London merchants, the expedition consisted of two ships, the *Primrose* and the *Lion*, and a pinnace called the *Moon*. They were manned by a crew of 140 men 'of the lustiest sort.' The captain of the *Lion* was Thomas Wyndham, leader of the expedition; the captain of the Primrose was a Portuguese pilot, experienced in the Guinea trade, named Antonio Anes Pinteado. When they arrived at the Portuguese fortress of La Mina, in what is now Ghana, they loladed 150 lb. of gold, then started following the coast eastward to Benin for a cargo of pepper. The more experienced Pinteado suggested that they return home before they were exposed to the dreaded heat of an equatorial summer. Wyndham, however, ignored that very sound advice. When Pinteado insisted on returning home, Wyndham persuaded him to stay by threatening to cut off his ears and nail them to the mast. On the Benin coast, they collected 80 tons of pepper over the next couple of months; they scurried homeward only when the men were dying of fever at the rate of four or five each day. Wyndham himself died on the homeward voyage. Of the 140 men who set out on the expedition, barely forty returned to Plymouth. Among the survivors was a young lad named Martin Frobisher.

At the same time that Wyndham was leading his tragic but very profitable expedition to West Africa, another English party was sailing into the mists of northern Norway in search of a northeast passage to the riches of the orient. This expedition consisted of three vessels, but only one, the *Edward Bonaventure* under captain Richard Chancellor, managed to get as far as the mouth of the Dvina River in the White Sea. From there he travelled by sled to Moscow, where he established diplomatic relations with the court of Czar Ivan IV. As a result of Chancellor's efforts, the first direct trade between England and Russia was established. The importance of that trade can hardly be over-emphasized, for England's continuing prosperity depended upon finding a constantly expanding market for her manufactured goods, particularly her woolens. The need for expanding markets, however, was not her only problem at the time. She was also threatened with serious civil disorder because of the number of unemployed and destitute people who were wandering around the country.

Humphrey Gilbert (1576), who later established Britain's first North American colony when he landed at St. John's in 1563, had a solution for both of England's problems. He suggested that new routes to the orient be sought out, and that overseas colonies should be established along such routes. 'We might inhabite some parte of those Countreys,' he pointed out, 'and settle there suche people of our Countrie, which now trouble the common welth, and through want here at home, are inforced to commit outragious offences, whereby they are dayly consumed with the Gallowes' (p. 160).

Waxing even more eloquent he pointed out that such a plan would have other benefits as well. It would, he suggested,

> have occasion, to set poor mens children to learne handie craftes, and therby to make trifles and such like, which the Indians and those people doe muche esteeme: By reason wherof, there should be none occasion, to have our countrey combred with loyterers, vagabonds, and such like idle persons (p. 160).

The need for overseas outlets—or 'vents,' as they were called at the time—had been widely discussed for at least a generation or two before Gilbert penned his famous lines. And there were other considerations as well. One of the problems that had to be solved before England could consider herself a serious contender in the struggle for overseas trade was the matter of navigation. English pilots could work their way along the coasts of Europe and Africa, but once they were off the continental shelf they were lost. The overseas voyages of the Spaniards and Portuguese were made possible by their knowledge of the new navigation. For the ancient system of following the coastline from headland to headland and feeling your way across the continental shelf with a lead-line was of no assistance whatever in finding your way across the broad expanses of the ocean seas. For that, a pilot needed to understand celestial navigation. He needed to be skilled in the use of the the astrolabe and the cross-staff, and to know enough astronomy to work out his latitude by measuring the elevation of the sun or the north star above the horizon. And these were not subjects that could be learned at sea in the same way that seamanship was learned from an experienced master. An illiterate seaman could learn the ways of a ship and with experience, could come to recognize familiar landmarks under a wide range of light and weather conditions; but the new navigation was a totally different matter, requiring the ability to read and write and use mathematical tables, and at least a smattering of navigational astronomy. These can be formidable subjects even today. To the sixteenth century seaman they were a complete mystery.

Realizing the problem they faced, the English merchants induced Sebastian Cabot to resign from his position as Chief Pilot of Spain, and to return to England in 1548. There he set about training navigators in the mysteries of celestial navigation. By that time, the merchants were interested mainly in developing the very profitable White Sea trade with Russia. By 1555, they were incorporated as *The Company of Merchants Adventurers of England for the Discovery of Lands, Territories, Isles, Dominions, and Seignories unknown,* usually referred to simply as the *Muscovy Company.* A London merchant and ship owner, Michael Lok, was elected governor in 1577; Sebastian Cabot was the chief pilot. Although the Muscovy Company was concentrating on the White Sea trade, they had never lost sight of their original goal—to find a new passage to the spice-laden islands of the South Pacific. And they reminded anyone who dared to challenge them, that they held the exclusive rights to carry on exploration to the northwest, the north, and the northeast.

—Walter Kenyon

## Martin Frobisher, 1576

THE FIRST PERSON TO SERIOUSLY CHALLENGE their authority was Martin Frobisher, whom we last met as a young lad on the Wyndham-Pinteado expedition to West Africa. Frobisher had been convinced for several years that he could locate a navigable passage around the northern end of North America, but had been unable to arrange the finances that were required to put his theory to the test. Finally, however, he caught the attention of Ambrose Dudley, Earl of Warwick, who agreed to apply political pressure against the Muscovy Company and its monopoly. Warwick argued that the Company should either undertake the search for a northwest passage itself, or permit another qualified party to do so. After a few brief but pointed political exchanges, Frobisher and his associates were granted the necessary license in February, 1575. Michael Lok, the London merchant who was still active in the Muscovy Company, agreed to raise the necessary funds for the expedition. Because Lok found it difficult to raise money at the time, the expedition was not ready to sail until the following

Meanwhile, they built the *Gabriel*, a small bark of twenty-five tons, and purchased another one that was even smaller, the 20-ton *Michael* (Collinson, 1867, p. 71). In contemporary terminology, a bark was a small, three-masted vessel that carried six sails: a course or mainsail and a topsail on both the mainmast and the foremast, a triangular sail called a lateen on the mizzenmast, and a small, rectangular spritsail slung on a yard underneath the bowsprit. Even these small vessels, however, were considered too large for inshore exploration. For such work, it was customary for one of the larger vessels on an expedition to carry a pinnace, a full rigged ship, but on a much smaller scale. To save space, pinnaces were usually carried in frame. That is, the timbers and planking were cut to size, but were not assembled until they were needed for inshore work at the end of the voyage. Because neither the *Gabriel* nor the *Michael* was large enough to carry his pre-fabricated

**Figure 1** Portrait in oils of Sir Martin Frobisher (1539-1594), attributed to the Dutch artist Cornelis Ketel (1548-1616), late 16th century. Courtesy of the Curators of the Bodleian Library, Oxford.

pinnace, Frobisher proposed to sail her across the North Atlantic on her own bottom. She was a tiny vessel of something less than ten tons, about the same size as Joshua Slocum's *Spray*, and carried a crew of four.

On 15 June 1576, the first Frobisher expedition set sail from Blackwell. Far to the northwest, after an uneventful passage, they 'hadde sighte of a highe and ragged lande,' but were unable to get near it because of the heavy ice and thick fog. They were probably off the southeast coast of Greenland at the time. A short while later, the fleet was scattered by a heavy gale. It knocked the topmast off the *Gabriel*, but Frobisher was able to repair the damage. The pinnace, however, was apparently lost with all hands, for it was never seen again. And the *Michael* was so severely damaged that her captain, Gryffyn Owen, decided to return to England. But the 'worthy captain, notwithstanding these discomfortes, continued hys course towards the north-weast, knowing that the sea at length must needes have an endyng, and that some lands should have a beginning that way.'

Frobisher's persistence was rewarded on 20 July when he sighted a high bluff that he named Queen Elizabeth's Foreland, on what is known today as Resolution Island. Shaping his course to the north, he raised another cape, which he named the North Foreland. Between the two was a broad passage leading to the west. Heavy ice and contrary winds prevented him from entering the passage for several days. On 11 July, when weather and ice conditions improved, he landed on Little Hall Island at the mouth of the passage, then sailed 'above fiftie leagues' into what he had decided was a strait. He described the strait as an open channel with Asia on its right side, and America on its left side.

Going ashore deep in the strait, he climbed a hill from which he saw a number of small objects floating far out to sea. He decided that they were 'porposes or seales, or some kinde of strange fishe.' As they drew nearer, however, he found that they were men in 'small boates made of leather.' Frobisher had made contact with the Baffin Island Eskimo.

At first, the relationship between the Europeans and the Eskimo was quite cordial. Frobisher and his men were astonished to see the natives eating raw meat and fish with such evident pleasure, and admired the strength and agility with which they climbed about in the ship's rigging. Bells and mirrors were traded for bear and seal-skin clothing to the satisfaction of all concerned. After mutual trust had been established through a series of such meetings, five of the seamen rowed ashore in the ship's boat to visit with their Eskimo friends; but they were 'intercepted with theyr boate, and were never since hearde of to this daye againe.'

Frobisher was now in an awkward position, for he had lost his only ship's boat. He had no way, therefore, of rescuing his men. Nor was he able to carry out any further inshore exploration. When he had first landed on Little Hall Island, Frobisher had asked his men to pick up any interesting objects that they could find. These were to be his 'tokens of possession,' proof that he had actually visited some strange land, and had claimed it for his sovereign. He had thus collected an assortment of odd-coloured rocks, tufts of grass, and similar mundane objects. He also had the skin clothing he had received in trade with the Eskimo. Among such objects, the clothing made from polar bear skins would have been particularly valuable in proving that he had visited some arctic land. But what he really wanted was one of the natives and his 'leather boate.' The natives were rather wary by that time, however, and refused to approach the ship. To lure them into captivity, Frobisher started ringing bells—which the natives greatly fancied. When one of the 'subtile traytours,' as Frobisher called them, finally paddled up to the side of the vessel to take the bell from the captain's hand, 'he was thereby taken himself; for'the captain being redily provided, let the bel fal and cought the man fast, and plucked him with maine force boate and al into his bark out of the sea.'

When Frobisher returned to England, his captive proved to

be a sensation. For he was 'a strange Infidel, whose like was never seen, red, nor harde of before, and whose language was neyther knowne nor understoode of anye.' Frobisher told his backers that the strait he had discovered almost certainly continued through to the Pacific Ocean, and that the northwest passage had to all intents and purpose been found. But then a strange thing happened. Frobisher gave Michael Lok a piece of rock as a souvenir. It was a 'peece of black stone, much lyke to a sea cole in coloure, whiche by the waight seemed to be some kinde of mettall or mynerall.' Lok sent it to a goldfiner—or an assayer, as we would call him today—to test for precious metals. The assayer reported that the rock contained gold, and in appreciable quantities.

With that magic word at their disposal, Lok and his associates immediately started planning for a second voyage.

Because the financial prospects of the 1577 voyage looked particularly bright, the merchants and venturers decided that they should be organized in some more formal manner. An application to the crown was favourably received, and, on 17 March, a charter was granted to them as 'The Adventurers to the Northwest for the Discovery of a Northwest Passage.' They were subsequently known, usually, as 'The Company of Cathay.' The new organization was a joint stock company modelled after the Levant and Muscovy companies. At a London meeting, the stockholders elected Michael Lok as governor, and appointed Martin Frobisher to the position of High Admiral of Cathay, as well as all newly discovered lands and seas. Heading the list of prominent merchants and courtiers who supported the second voyage was Queen Elizabeth herself, who subscribed £ 1,000. The total number of venturers was forty-one; the total subscription was £ 4,275.

The focus, however, had shifted. Although a more thorough exploration of the strait might be undertaken, the primary purpose of the next expedition was to be gold-mining. Frobisher was to sail directly to Little Hall Island, where the 'peece of black stone' had been picked up the previous year, and load the ships with as much of the ore as they could safely carry. Only when the mines were in full operation, and a safe anchorage had been found for the ships, was Frobisher to look for the five men he had lost on the previous expedition, and continue his exploration of the strait. For this voyage, the *Gabriel* and the *Michael* were refitted, and the support of Queen Elizabeth I was enlisted. She agreed to loan the merchants one of her tall ships, the *Ayde*, of some 200 tons. This was to be a well equipped expedition with a complement of 141 men, including soldiers, miners and assayers, as well as sailors to man the ships.

## Martin Frobisher, 1577

THE SMALL FLEET SAILED FROM BLACKWALL on 26 May 1577. Sailing north up the east coast of England and Scotland, they stopped at the Orkney Islands to lay in some fresh provisions. Frobisher and his men were not at all impressed with the Orkneys. They described the islands as 'much subject to colde, answerable to such a climate, and yet yeeldeth some frutes, and sufficient mayntenance for the people contented so poorly to live. Their houses are but poore without, and sluttish ynough within, and the people in nature thereunto agreeable' (Kenyon, 1975, p. 47).

On 8 June, they again headed out to sea. Twenty six days later they raised the ice-bound coast of Greenland, after an uneventful passage. Frobisher tried to go ashore there, as he had tried during his first voyage, but was again prevented from doing so by the heavy ice that lay along the coast. Abandoning the attempt after four days, he shaped his course for the strait. He landed on Little Hall Island, where he had found the ore the previous year, but was unable to find any more. The assayers did find rich deposits, however, on Hall Island, as well as on the other small islands in the area. While they were on Hall Island they met with the natives, with neither party trusting the other, and with good reason. The Eskimo had taken five of Frobisher's mariners the previous year; and the English were hoping to capture one of the natives to train as an interpreter. The English were finally successful. After a brief struggle, they took one of the natives, and carried him aboard the *Ayde.*

Hoping to find a safe anchorage, Frobisher then moved the vessels to the south shore of the strait. After cruising about for a couple of days, they entered an inlet that they named Jackman's Sound after Charles Jackman, masters mate aboard the *Ayde.* They found many traces of 'gold' in the sound, but not in sufficient quantity to justify mining. They did, however, find a dead narwhal on the shore of a small island. It was described as 'a great deade fishe . . . in proportion rounde like a porpose, being about twelve foote long, and in bigness answerable, havying a horne of two yardes long growing out of the snoute or nostrels. This horne,'he said, 'is wreathed and stryte, like in fashion to a taper made of waxe, and may truely be thoughte to be the sea Unicorn.' But it was now 26 July, and Frobisher had little time to dawdle over dead unicorns, intriguing though they were. He decided, therefore, to leave the *Ayde* in Jackson Sound, where it was relatively safe, and seek out some large deposit of ore with the two barks.

The same night, they dropped their anchors in a deep sound back on the north shore of the strait. They named it Beare Sound after James Beare, master of the *Michael.* As soon as they were ashore, they found a very rich ore deposit, and set the miners to work. But the tides swept such vast quantities of ice into the sound that they were forced to put to sea, leaving behind some 20 tons of ore that had already been collected. Then they headed up the strait, looking for a safer anchorage. About 15 miles farther west, they discovered another that was well protected from drifting ice by a string of small islands. On one of the small islands within the sound, quite near to where they had anchored, they found a very rich deposit of ore. Again, Frobisher set his miners to work. The next day he sent the *Michael* to bring the *Ayde* to the newly discovered harbour,

**Figure 2** An Inuit hunter in a kayak, wielding the three-pronged spear used for seabirds and fish; another hunter on the shore with kayak and bow-and-arrow; an Inuit woman with a child in the hood of her parka; a summer camp in the background. Woodcut published in George Beste's *A True Discourse of the Late Voyages of Discoverie, for the Finding of a Passage to Cathaia* (London, 1578), after a drawing by John White (c. 1540-5-flg. 1593), a British artist who was probably a member of Frobisher's 1577 expedition to South Baffin Island. Courtesy, The Hakluyt Society, London.

which, like the gold-bearing island, he named after the Countess of Warwick, wife of Ambrose Dudley, Earl of Warwick.

On the way to Jackman Sound, the *Michael* was becalmed, and carried by the tide into yet another sound on the south shore, later named Yorke Sound after Gilbert Yorke, the captain of the vessel. While he was lying there at anchor, he happened to notice a few skin tents of the natives, not too far away. When he and his men went ashore to investigate, they found that the natives had fled; but inside the tents they found some of the clothing of the men who had been taken the previous year. They found a canvas doublet, shirt, a belt, and 'three shoes for contrarie feete and of unequal bignesse.' Hoping to make contact with the captured sailors, Yorke left them a letter describing Frobisher's present whereabouts together with a pen, a bottle of ink, and some writing-paper. He was hoping, of course, that the Englishmen were still alive, and might be able to send Frobisher a message as to their whereabouts. Leaving a few mirrors and similar small objects as a sign of friendship, they returned aboard the *Michael*, and sailed east to Jackman Sound, just a few miles away.

After discussing the matter at some length with the men aboard the *Ayde*, it was decided to launch a pincers attack on the native encampment in the hope of freeing their countrymen. One party, led by Jackman, would go overland to attack the encampment, while another party, led by Captain Yorke, would row up the coast and lie in ambush at the mouth of the sound, thus preventing the natives from escaping by sea. When Jackman arrived at the place where the tents had been the previous day, he found that they were gone. He kept working his way towards the mouth of the sound, however, and after climbing over 'two or three tedious mountains' he happened upon their new location.

There were some eighteen to twenty people in camp at the time. When they saw the Englishmen approaching their camp, the natives took to their boats, and headed out to sea. But

Jackman's men fired their muskets to alert their comrades who were waiting at the entrance to the sound for just such an eventuality. Seeing that their escape by sea was cut off, the natives landed on a point of land on the west side of the sound, with their pursuers close behind them. The natives defended themselves as well as they could, but were no match for the English. Five or six of the natives were slaughtered; several escaped overland; and only the mortally wounded remained. These, 'being ignorant of what mercy meaneth, with deadly furie they cast themselves headlong from off the rock into the sea, least perhaps their enemies shoulde receive glory or praye of their dead carcasses.' Surveying the field of battle—known since as Bloody Point—the English found two native women hiding among the boulders. 'One being old and ougly, our men thought she had been a divell or some witch, and therefore let her go.' The other was a young woman 'combred with a sucking childe at hir back.' This one they kept.

By 6 August, mining on the Countess of Warwick Island was well in hand. The soldiers were stationed on shore to protect the miners, and had fortified the place as well as they could. The natives appeared from time to time on the mainland opposite the island, probably at Tikkoon Point. But no further hostilities broke out. The miners 'brought aboorde almost twoo hundereth tunne of golde ore, in the space of twentie dayes.' They finished work on 21 August, well satisfied with the results they had achieved. In any event, it was time to leave. For about that time, as Best (1578) records, 'ye ise began to congeale and freese about our ships sides a night, whiche gave us a good argument of the sunnes declyning southwarde, and put us in minde to make more haste homeward.' The next day they built a bonfire near the centre of the Island, then fired 'a vollie of shotte for a farewell, in honour of the right Honourable Lady Anne, Countesse of Warwick, whose name it beareth, and so departed aboorde.'

As soon as the ore was unloaded, at Bristol and Dartford, new assays were run. This time, the results were truly spectacular. One assayer reported that a ton of ore contained precious metals to the value of £67.1.8 Another assay reported a value of £53.10.3 per ton. Juggling such figures was an intoxicating exercise. It was calculated, for example, that an expedition capable of bringing back 2,000 tons of ore could be mounted for £20, 836.13.4. And that quantity or ore would yield a gross return of at least £60,000, or a net profit of £39,163.6.8. But first, they had to build smelters in which to extract the gold and silver form its matrix. The Company decided to set up two smelters, one at Bristol, the other at 'St. Katheryns hyll,' the Dartford residence of Sir William Winter, one of the merchants. By 19 January, they were working on the Dartford smelter, which was 84 feet long and 36 feet wide (Collinson, p. 171). It had water-driven stamping mills to crush the ore, and three furnaces, one for roasting, and two for smelting. Each furnace was equipped with a bellows. Michael Lok reported at the time that the smelting would be completed in six or eight weeks.

Lok's prediction is of some interest in that it is the first time, apparently, that a specific schedule was set down. Prior to that time, the assayers had been extremely cautious in that regard. While they had turned in glowing reports as to the high concentration of gold and silver in the ore, they had not yet managed to produce any. This, they suggested—but didn't exactly say—was due to the inadequacy of the equipment with which they were forced to work. But by and large, they avoided specific statements as to what *was* required. Lok's comment, then, suggests that someone was beginning to ask awkward questions, questions that could not really be answered. It is possible, of course, that Lok had some information that does not appear in the record. In the light of subsequent events, however, it is difficult to accept such an explanation. It is much more likely, in fact, that he and his associates were simply carried away by one of the waves of excitement and cupidity that periodically batter down the fragile structures of human reason. That is, we must attribute their behaviour to 'gold

**Figure 3** Frobisher's men in a skirmish with Inuit at Bloody Point, 1 August 1577, with an Inuit in a kayak in the foreground, and an encampment of sealskin tents on a hilltop in the far upper-left. Drawing by the British physician and collector Dr. Hans Sloane (1660-1753), after an original watercolour by John White. Courtesy of the Trustees of the British Museum, London.

fever' rather than to any rational processes.

In spite of the fact that the Company of Cathay was seriously in debt, their plans for a third voyage to the northwest were already well advanced. This was to be a major expedition with 15 ships and a complement of some 400 men. Frobisher's third voyage, incidentally, is still the largest arctic expedition that has ever been fielded. By that time, the search for a northwest passage was virtually forgotten. Frobisher was instructed to sail directly to the Countess of Warwick Sound. There, he was to set his miners to work on the ore deposits that had already been found. Only when the mining was going smoothly was he to explore the area more thoroughly, and perhaps find even richer veins of precious metals. He was also instructed to establish a settlement of 100 men who were to spend the winter mining and stockpiling ore. The wintering-party, led by Captain Edward Fenton, consisted of 30 miners, 30 soldiers and forty sailors, gunners, shipwrights and carpenters. To house the wintering-party, the ships carried a prefabricated structure that was probably a fort. It is described as 'a howse of timber heare framed for our lodginge and storehowses conteyning 132 foote in length and 72 foote in breadthe with ii (bastions or flankers?) at either ende thereof' (Taylor, 1980, p. 192fn.). Three of the vessels, the *Gabriel, Michael* and *Judith,* were to spend the winter in the Countess of Warwick Sound with Fenton's party. The other vessels, richly laden with the choicest ore, were to return to England at the end of the summer.

## Martin Frobisher, 1578

THE THIRD FROBISHER EXPEDITION to the land that Queen Elizabeth I had named *Meta Incognita* sailed from Harwich on 31 May 1578. Six days later, off the southern coast of Ireland, they paused to assist some Bristol sailors whose small bark had been attacked by pirates a few days before. Frobisher provided them 'with surgerie and salves, to heale their hurtes, and with meate and drinke to comfort their pining harts.'

As he shaped his course to the west-and-by-north, Frobisher eventually found that he was being pushed off course by a steady current that swept across the north Atlantic from the Bay of Mexico to the coast of Norway. His observation is among the earliest references to the Gulf Stream.

On 20 June, three weeks out of Harwich, the fleet raised the coast of Greenland. Frobisher and some of the officers went ashore near Cape Farewell, at the southern tip of the island. Because they were 'the fyrste known Christians that we have true notice of, that ever set foote upon that ground,' Frobisher formally claimed it for England. While they were ashore, they happened upon an abandoned native camp-site. The Eskimo, had seen the Englishmen coming, no doubt, and had prudently taken to the hills. After examining the gear that was lying about, Frobisher decided, correctly, that the natives of Greenland and the natives of Meta Incognita were the same people. Inside one of the tents, Frobisher's men found a 'boxe of nayles and a tryvet of yron.' They concluded that the natives of Greenland must 'have trade with some civill people, or else are in deede themselves artificiall workemen.'

By 5 July, the English had forced their vessels through heavy streams of ice, and arrived off the mouth of the strait. But the strait was 'frosen over from one side to the other, and heavy walles, mountaines, and bulwarkes of yse, choaked uppe the passage, and denied us entrance.' At this point in the narrative, Best pauses, as he does from time to time, to comment on the fact that ice-bergs are formed from fresh water rather than salt water. He realized that they must therefore have been formed on land, but beyond that, he could not go. The mighty Greenland ice-cap that spawns such incredible numbers of bergs had not yet been discovered by western Europeans.

The weather at that point became particularly foul. With the wind settled firmly in the east, more and more ice was packed in against the ships. Then fog and snow were added to their problems, making it increasingly difficult for the vessels to remain together, or to come to each other's assistance. In fact, the fleet was already partly dispersed before it entered the ice. For neither the *Judith* nor the *Michael* had been seen for some three weeks. And now they were hit by a storm that threatened to sink them all. Each ship did what it could to protect itself from the encroaching ice. The men hung ropes, timbers and beds, as well as spare masts and yards over the sides of their ships to fend off the slabs of ice that were literally squeezing the vessels out of shape. There was only one casualty, however, the 100-ton *Dennis*, which was nipped in the ice and sunk. Under the circumstances, there was really very little that the men could do to protect themselves. Ultimately, as Best pointed out, 'they were fayne to submit themselves and their ships to the mercie of the unmerciful ise.'

But even arctic storms must end. When the wind finally shifted to the northwest, the ice and fogs rapidly dispersed, allowing the battered ships to gain sea-room. There they licked their wounds, plugging leaks, setting up fallen top-masts, and making general repairs. This done, they took in their sails, and lay quietly adrift.

The next day, the scattered fleet again headed west till they picked up what they thought was the North Foreland. As they sailed into the strait, however, the land seemed strangely unfamiliar. The pilots discussed the matter among themselves, but could not arrive at a consensus. Some insisted that they were in Frobisher Strait, but that the land looked different because most of the familiar landmarks had been obliterated by the heavy fall of snow. Others maintained—and with equal emphasis—that they had entered a totally different strait, and that Frobisher Strait was farther north. After sailing some 200 miles into what they called the Mistaken Strait, they finally realized their error, and headed back for Davis Strait. When they arrived at the Countess of Warwick Sound, they found their two missing vessels, the *Judith* and the *Michael*, riding quietly at anchor. To celebrate the reunion, the Reverend Mr.

Wolfall 'made unto them a godly sermon, exhorting them especially to be thankefull to God for theyr strange and miraculous deliverance in those so dangerous places.'

Although the *Anne Frances*, the *Thomas of Ipswich* and the *Moone* were still scattered along the coast of Resolution Island, Frobisher started work the next day. Tents, picks and shovels, crow-bars and provisions were carried ashore, where the miners immediately started digging out ore. Soldiers patrolled the island to protect the workers from marauding natives. Kitchens were set up to prepare meals; and assayers and blacksmiths rigged up their furnaces and forges. It was a busy but well organized operation. As the miners dug the ore out of the ground, it was loaded into baskets, carried to the shore, then loaded aboard the small boats that carried it out to the nearby ships. On 28 August, the missing vessels arrived at the Countess of Warwick Sound, battered, but still afloat.

By that time, the surrounding area had been thoroughly explored, and a number of rich ore-bodies were being worked. Apart from the two quarries on the Countess of Warwick Island, the men were working on the Countess of Sussex Island, at Sabine Bay, a few miles up the coast, on Newland Island, in Beares Sound and in Dyers Passage, the modern Victoria Bay. When the last ship sailed from the Countess of Warwick Sound on 1 September, 1578, the fleet was laden with 1,350 tons of ore that was believed to be richly laced with gold and silver.

Frobisher and his officers had long since abandoned the idea of founding a settlement along that barren coast. And in any event, half of their prefabricated house had been lost with the *Dennis*. However, Captain Taylor did erect a small building at the highest point on the island to see if it would survive the winter. The house was 14 feet long and 8 feet wide; it was build of stone rubble set in mortar, and had a wooden roof (Taylor, 1980, p. 198). The surviving sections of the prefabricated structure, together with some of the anvils and supplies, were buried on the island. Other gear was buried on the Countess of Sussex Island. And so they departed homeward, sailing southwest-by-south from the Queen's Foreland, 'which was the best course we colde holde for 200 leagues to passe into warmer climate.'

When he arrived back in England, Frobisher found that the Company of Cathay's treasury was empty. There was not even enough cash on hand to pay off the crews of his ships. Thomas Allen had replaced Michael Lok as treasurer of the company by that time, but he voiced the same complaint; as treasurer, he saw very little treasure. One problem was that the smelters had not yet produced any gold from the huge stock-pile of ore. The assayers talked, argued, and complained about the difficulties they faced in trying to work with inferior equipment, but they produced no tangible results. It was this lack of results that led directly to the second problem, the fact that the shareholders had failed to put up the money that, in more sanguine times, they had agreed to advance. On paper, the company's finances were in reasonably good shape. The officers of the company therefore petitioned the Queen to intercede on their behalf, to force the reluctant shareholders to meet their financial obligations.

The Queen agreed to act on the company's petition, and authorized Michael Lok to collect the £6,000 that were outstanding (Collinson, 1867, p. 320). The shareholders, however preferred to discuss the matter, rather than surrender their hard cash. For example, they asked for a complete accounting for the three voyages, then questioned almost every expense. Michael Lok, on the other hand, had spent at least £4,920 on the company's behalf and wanted to be reimbursed. Lok's expenditure amounted to almost a quarter of the £20,160 that the company had spent on the three voyages. These were vast sums of money in an age in which it cost the company only £83 to build the *Gabriel* for the first voyage; the pinnace that was built at the same time cost only £20 (Collinson, 1867, p. 115). Lok's investment, then, was a substantial one. He may, however, have been exaggerating when pleading his case before the privy council. But he did inform them that they had

**Figure 4** Engraved portrait of Martin Frobisher, from Richard Hakluyt's *The Principall Navigations Voiages & Discoveries of the English Nation...* (London, 1589), a photo-lithographic facsimile of which was published by the Hakluyt Society, Cambridge in 1965. The Latin inscription reads: 'Joyfully Frobisher travelled Neptune's kingdoms for his country but finally met his death when struck by a missile' (i.e. in action against the Spanish at Crozon in 1594). Courtesy, The Hakluyt Society, London.

invested 'all the goodes that he hath in the world without exception; wherby now hym sellf and wyfe and fifteen children are left in state to beg their bread hensforthe' (Collinson, 1867, p. 350).

Gold-rushes are strange but predictable phenomena. They invariably start with feverish activity, for they are fuelled with a highly inflammable mixture of ambition and greed. Expectations are escalated with such astonishing speed that reason gets left far behind. If gold is actually present, as it was in California and the Yukon, for example, fortunes may be made overnight. For most of the miners, however, things do not 'pan out,' as they say. But the hopes never end as abruptly as they began; they fade out slowly, pushed slowly into the background by an encroaching reality that clamours for attention. And if gold is *not* present, as was the case with the Frobisher mines, the result is exactly the same. The process starts with feverish activity, then slowly tapers off as man learns once again that 'all is not gold that shineth.'

With the Company of Cathay, the northwest venture flared up suddenly, as we have seen. Then, when it slowly became obvious that the whole thing was a delusion, the merchants and seamen turned to their charts and globes, which led them back to their original scheme. What had drawn the English to the far northwest, was, after all, not gold, but the expectation of finding a northwest passage to the riches of the far east, of Japan, China, and the spice islands. And when the gold-fever finally subsided, the original purpose was revived.

Joint stock companies of the period were loose associations of people, mainly merchants, who bought shares in a single trading venture. At the end of a successful venture, the profits were distributed among the share-holders. If the venture was not successful, the venturers were expected to assume responsibility for any outstanding debts or obligations. Such joint stock companies differed from modern trading companies or corporations in that they made no provision for amassing funds in the company treasury. For at the end of a venture, the profits—all of them—were distributed among the shareholders. The next venture then started from scratch. It might or might not have the same list of subscribers. Usually, the leaders of such a venture petitioned the crown to grant them a trading monopoly in any newly discovered lands, or along any newly discovered trade routes. Throughout the early period of English exploration, there was a bewildering number of such stock companies, with each such flurry of activity dominated by a particular individual. Michael Lok, as we have seen, was the dominant figure behind the Frobisher voyages.

The next group to take up the search for a northwest passage was led by William Sanderson, a wealthy merchant who was married to Sir Walter Raleigh's niece. Sanderson was a prominent member of the Fishmongers' Guild of London. And it was he, apparently, who selected John Davis, 'a man very well grounded in the principles of navigation, for captaine and chief pilot of the exployt.' Although Sanderson was a London merchant himself, well over half of the funds subscribed for Davis's first voyage were put up by the merchants of Devon.

## John Davis, 1585

DAVIS SAILED FROM DARTMOUTH on 7 June 1585, with two small vessels, the *Sunneshine* and the *Moonshine*. Davis himself sailed aboard the *Sunneshine*, a 50-ton bark, with a complement of twenty-three men; the thirty-five-ton *Moonshine* was under the command of Captain William Bruton. In addition to the usual complement of officers and men, the expedition was provided with a gunner, four musicians, and a merchant named John Jane. Jane, the nephew of Sanderson, was presumably aboard to watch over the interests of the venturing merchants. He also wrote the report on the first voyage, and later on, the third (Markham, 1880, p. xvii-xxvii).

Shortly after leaving Dartmouth, the wind shifted to the

west, forcing the vessels to put into Falmouth, and then into the Scilly Islands. It was not until 28 June that they were finally able to leave England under a fair east wind. When they were south of Iceland, Davis reported seeing large numbers of whales; it was this sighting, incidentally, that was to lead to the development of the very lucrative whale fishery in that area. On the nineteenth, they ran into heavy streams of ice that were drifting south along the east coast of Greenland. Staying outside the ice, they headed north to see if they could sail around Greenland that way. But adverse winds forced them to turn south, and follow the coast. Davis was probably off Cape Discord at the time, or about 61° north. He described that coast as 'the most deformed rocky and mountainous land that ever we sawe.'

Clearing Cape Farewell at the bottom tip of Greenland, they followed the coast to the northwest. The men were apparently becoming restless, perhaps as a result of ice and weather conditions off a strange and forbidding coast. To cheer them up, Davis increased their rations. He ordered that 'every messe being five persons, shall have halfe a pound of bread and a kan of beere every morning at breakfast.' The men, however, thought that the rations were still inadequate, and convinced Davis to increase it again. This time he raised the daily ration for each mess of five men to 4 pounds of bread, 12 quarts of beer, 6 'neweland fishes' (probably Newfoundland cod), and on flesh days an additional gill of peas. At the same time, he reduced the men's allowance of butter and cheese. Davis did not record the number of 'flesh days' there were in a week; nor does he tell us what kind of flesh was being served. From other accounts of the period, however, we may assume that there would have been three or four flesh days per week, and that the meat would have been mainly salt beef.

Davis and his men first went ashore on an island in the mouth of what is now Godthåb Fjord in Greenland. They learned for the first time that the country was inhabited when they found bits of fur clothing on the beach. Davis and two of his officers climbed to the top of a hill, from which they were seen by the natives. The English only learned of the natives' presence when the latter 'made a lamentable noise, as we thought, with great outcryes and screechings; wee hearing them, thought it had bene howling wolves.' Captain Bruton, meanwhile, had seen the natives approaching the shore-party, and hurried ashore himself with a group of armed men and the four musicians. Bruton was prepared, as Davis tells us, 'either by force to rescue us, if neede should so require, or with curtesie to allure the people.' As the natives cautiously approached them, the musicians started playing their instruments, and the sailors started dancing. The natives were apparently entranced by these strange antics, but remained at a prudent distance throughout.

The following day, when the Eskimo were less apprehensive, the English were able to purchase five kayaks, and a variety of paddles, spears and clothing, fashioned from both seal-skins and bird-skins. Davis was astonished at the amount of wood that the Eskimo had, but could not find out where it came from. He was equally intrigued by the quantity of driftwood that he encountered on both the east and west coasts of Greenland. He decided, finally, that it must have come from somewhere in the interior; for the only wood that seemed to grow along the coast was dwarf birch and willow, and these were nothing more than shrubs. (It was another 200 years before man learned that the driftwood along the Greenland coast originated in Siberia). In describing the islands where he landed, Davis remarked that 'the cliffes were al of such oare as M. Frobisher brought from meta Incognita.'

The explorers left Greenland on 1 August, shaping their course to the northwest. Five days later they raised the coast of what is now Baffin Island, and dropped their anchors in a deep inlet they named Exeter Sound. On entering the sound, they passed between two bold capes: the one on the north side of the entrance they named Cape Dyer; the one on the south they named Cape Walsingham, after Sir Francis, their chief patron.

These names, incidentally, are still in use, as is the name 'Mount Raleigh,' chosen for a peak on the north shore of Exeter Sound.

Shortly after they arrived at their anchorage—which they named ''Totnes Road'—the men noticed some animals on shore. Davis describes the ensuing scene as follows:

> We supposing them to bee goates or wolves, manned out boats, and went towards them; but when wee came neere the shore, wee found them to be white beares of a monstruous bignesse: we being desirious of fresh victual and the sport, began to assault them, and I being on land one of them came down the hil right against me; my piece was charged with haileshot and a bullet, tooke the water straight, making smal account of his hurt. Then we followed him on our boate, and killed him with boare speares, and two more that night.

And thus ended the earliest recorded bear hunt in arctic Canada!

From Exeter Sound, they followed the coast south for some eighty niles, where they discovered another broad inlet, the present Cumberland Sound. The headland they rounded to enter the sound, they named the Cape of God's Mercy. Following the north shore deep into the sound, they discovered the Middleaktuk Islands, but did not bother to name them; nor did they name the sound itself. Davis and his men spent the next fifteen days exploring the sound, and had high hopes of finding a passage to the west. But it was late in the season, and the weather was deteriorating, so they decided to return home. Taking their departure from the Cape of God's Mercy, they headed southeast for England. A month later, on 30 September 1585, the vessels arrived back at Dartmouth.

Three days later, Davis sent an enthusiastic letter to Sir Francis Walsingham, secretary to the Privy Council. He assured Walsingham that 'the north-west passage is a matter nothing doubtfull, but at any tyme almost to be passed, the sea navigable, voyde of yse, the ayre tolerable, and the waters very depe.' In addition to finding what appeared to be the entrance to the northwest passage, he informed Sir Francis that he had also found 'an yle of very grate quantytie, not on any globe or map dyscrybed, yielding a sufficient trade of furre and leather (Markham, 1880:xix). Davis's important discoveries, backed by his obvious enthusiasm for the project, convinced the merchants that the search should be continued.

## John Davis, 1586

DAVIS LEFT ON HIS SECOND VOYAGE with a fleet of four vessels: the 120-ton *Mermayde,* the 50-ton *Sunneshine,* the 35-ton *Moonshine*(which Davis consistently miscalled the *Moonlight* , and a 10-ton pinnace called the *Northstarre.* They sailed from Dartmouth on 7 May 1586, passed the Scilly Isles, then coasted the south shore of Ireland before shaping their course to the northwest. It must have been an uneventful passage, for no details are recorded. We know from other sources, however, that two of the vessels the *Sunneshine* and the *Northstarre,* left the convoy on 7 June to explore the channel between Iceland and Greenland, Denmark Strait on a modern chart. After leaving England, Davis's first entry in the log of his voyage is dated 15 June. On that day he raised Cape Farewell, at the tip of Greenland. He recorded its position as 60° north and 47° west an amazingly accurate piece of navigation, considering the crude instruments he had to work with. He had hoped to go ashore there, but there was just too much ice along the coast. The ice was so thick, in fact, that he was forced to drop far to the south before he could make any westing. Pestered as he was with ice, snow and gales, he did not reach the west coast of Greenland for another two weeks. And then he was forced ashore by westerly winds.

He landed at a group of islands in the mouth of Godthåb Fjord, the inlet he had named Gilbert Sound on his previous visit. He described the coast as lying 'North Northwest and

South South Southeast, wee knowe not howe farre.' He decided that one of the islands would be a good place to set up the small pinnace he had carried in frame aboard the *Mermayde*, a vessel that he would use for inshore exploration. One of his first moves, therefore, was to send out some boats to locate a safe anchorage for the ships. When the Eskimo saw the English boats, they approached them most cautiously. Soon, however, they recognized some of the seamen who had been there the year before, 'and hung about the boate with such comfortable joy as woulde require a long discourse to be uttered.'

Later in the day, when the boats returned to the ships, Davis and the merchants—introduced here for the first time—went ashore. There were eighteen Eskimo in the group, and Davis gave each of them a knife. This was not actually a gift, but the first move in an economic transaction that is known to the anthropologists as 'gift exchange,' a widely used system among groups that have no recognized medium of exchange such as our money, for example.

The next day, when they started setting up the pinnace on a neighbouring island, large numbers of Eskimo again arrived to watch the strange proceedings. They assisted with the work from time to time, and set up a brisk trade with the merchants. For small items such as knives and bracelets, they traded seal skins, caribou skins, rabbits, seal meat, salmon, cod and dried capelin, 'with other fish and byrdes such as the country did yeelde.' While all this was going on, Davis sent out the ships' boats to explore the surrounding country. He warned the men that they were not to molest the natives; nor were they to remove anything from any native encampments or caches they might happen upon. On their return, the men reported finding 'a plaine champion countrey, with earth and grasse, such as our moory and waste grounds of England are.' This they found some ten miles in the interior, surrounded by snow-covered mountains. And on one of the islands near the mouth of the fjord, they found a grave marked with a wooden cross.

Although generations of historians have tried to figure out what Christians were buried there (for it was a multiple burial, covered only with seal skins), no one has yet found the answer. Perhaps they were some late survivors of the lost Viking settlements; or perhaps they were from some European vessel whose voyage to that isolated coast was never recorded. We still don't know.

Davis was intrigued by the Eskimo, and spent a great deal of time watching them and describing their various activities. He was particularly struck by the fact that they ate raw meat and fish with such obvious relish. Because the ships were anchored amid a cluster of islands, Davis only met the Eskimo men, those who could paddle out to the islands in a kayak. There is no reference to his meeting an Eskimo woman or child. He was deeply impressed, however, by the Eskimo men, and the skill with which they handled their skin-covered craft. He tells us, for example, that 'they are never out of the water, but live in the nature of fishes, but only when dead sleepe taketh them, and then under a warme rocke, lying his boat upon the land, he lyeth downe to sleepe.'

But all was not idyllic. The English soon found that the natives 'are very simple in theyr conversation but marvellous theevish, especially for iron.' In the beginning, the pilfering of the natives was more annoying than serious. But they became more bold with the passage of time, making of with a ship's boat, and finally an anchor. As a crowning indignity, they unleashed their slings, and peppered the English with stones. In retaliation, Davis captured one of the Eskimo, and dispersed the rest by firing off a small cannon. Later that day, 11 July, they weighed their anchors, and put to sea, shaping their course to the west. Six days later Davis encountered what the whalers of a later period would call the 'middle pack.'

Davis encountered the pack on 17 July at about 63° north. He had never before seen such a solid mass of floe ice, and thought at first that it was snow-covered land. With large bergs rising out of the fields of ice, his mistake was a natural one. He sent the pinnace ahead to explore the newly discovered land, and was astonished when she reported back that it was nothing but ice. The report 'bred great admiration in us all, considering the huge quantity thereof, incredible to be reported in truth as it was, and therefore I omit to speake any further therof.' Davis was sorely perplexed by the quantity of ice in the area because he had crossed the strait to Baffin Island at about the same latitude the year before with no trouble at all; and now he was stopped by a solid barrier of ice. He coasted the ice-front for the next thirteen days, but could find no opening.

There was neither rain nor snow reported during this period, but there was a dense fog that apparently lasted several days. The fog was so thick, in fact, that the moisture froze on the sails and rigging, shrouding the entire vessel in a thick layer of ice. The men became alarmed at their position, and 'very orderly and with good discretion' suggested that they turn back. Davis took their suggestion quite seriously, and recorded in the log that 'I should not through my over boldnesse leave their widowes and fatherlesse children to give me bitter curses.' Davis himself wanted to continue the exploration—or the discovery, as he called it—but at the same time, he realized that to continue with a disgruntled crew would probably be unwise. There was an obvious way out of the dilemma, however. He would return to the coast of Greenland, refit the *Mooneshine* for further exploration, and send the *Mermayde* back to England. As the men and officers agreed with the plan, he shaped his course to the east southeast, and two days later raised the coast of Greenland at 66°33' north.

While the *Mooneshine* was being refitted, the merchants carried on a brisk trade in furs. And at the same time, Davis sent the pinnace off to explore the surrounding country. Again, they found themselves amid a cluster of islands, separated by deep sounds. In this place, Davis reported, 'we found it very hot, and we were very much troubled with a flie which is called a Musketa, for they did sting grievously.' The natives, they found, were the same as those they had met earlier, in Gilbert

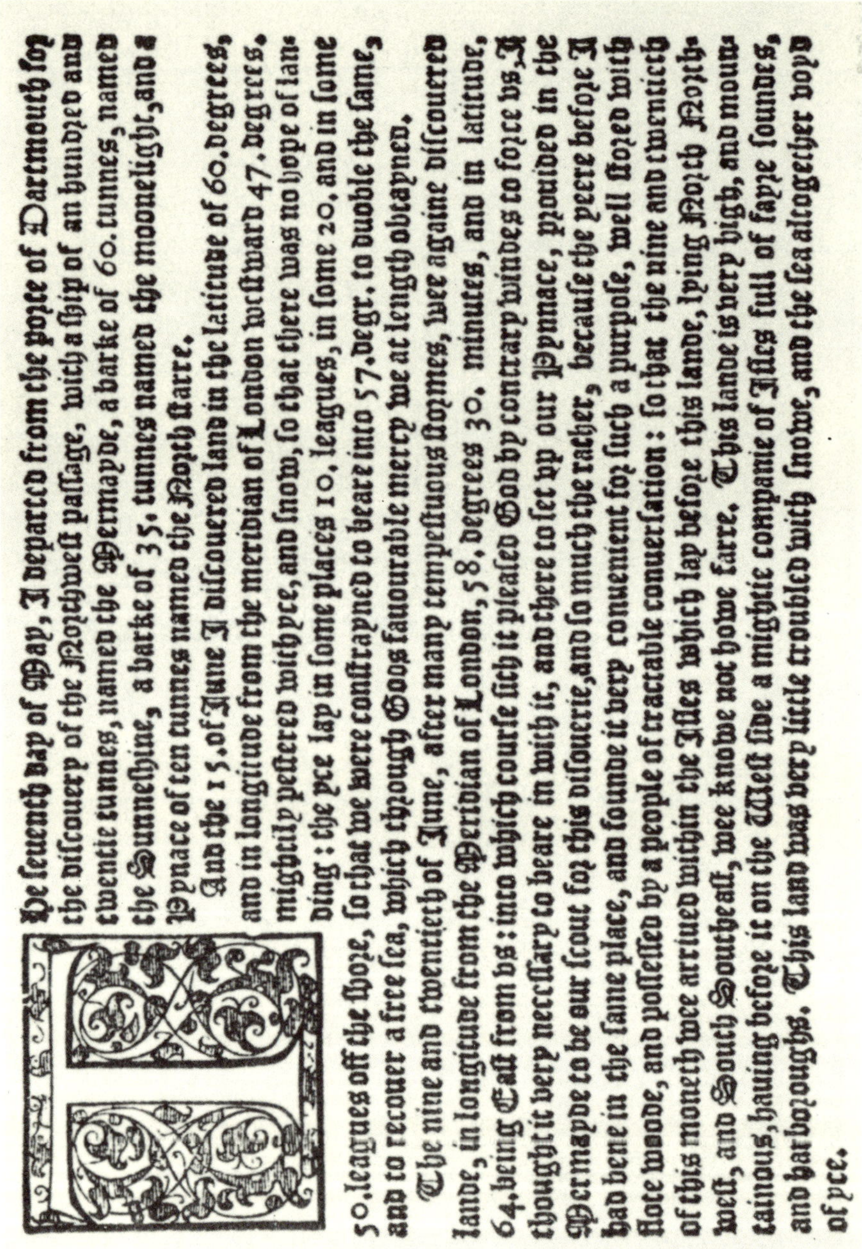

The seuenth day of May, I departed from the porte of Dartmouth for the discouery of the Northwest passage, with a ship of an hundred and twentie tunnes, named the Mermayde, a barke of 60. tunnes, named the Sunneshine, a barke of 35. tunnes named the moonelight, and a Pynace of ten tunnes named the North starre.

And the 15. of June I discouered land in the latitude of 60. degrees, and in longitude from the meridian of London westward 47. degrees, mightily pestered with yce, and snow, so that there was no hope of landing: the yce lay in some places 10. leagues, in some 20. and in some 50. leagues off the shore, so that we were constrayned to beare into 57. degr. to duoble the same, and to recouer a free sea, which through Gods fauourable mercy we at length obtayned.

The nine and twentieth of June, after many tempestuous stormes, wee againe discouered lande, in longitude from the Meridian of London, 58. degrees 30. minutes, and in latitude, 64. being East from vs: into which course sith it pleased God by contrary windes to force vs, I thought it very necessary to beare in with it, and there to set vp our Pynnace, prouided in the Mermayde to be our scout for this disouerie, and so much the rather, because the yeere before I had bene in the same place, and founde it very conuenient for such a purpose, well stored with flote woode, and possessed by a people of tractable conuersation: so that the nine and twentieth of this moneth wee arriued within the Isles which lay before this lande, lying North Northwest, and South Southeast, wee knowe not howe farre. This lande is very high, and mountainous, hauing before it on the West side a mightie companie of Isles full of fayre soundes, and harboroughs. This land was very little troubled with snowe, and the sea altogether voyd of yce.

**Figure 5** The first page of John Davis's account of his second Arctic voyage (1586), from Hakluyt's *Principall Navigations...* (London, 1589, first edition, second issue). Metropolitan Toronto Library.

Sound. When the refit was completed, eleven days later, Davis weighed his anchor, and headed due west in the *Mooneshine*, leaving the *Mermayde* and the pinnace riding at anchor in the sound.

Davis picked up the east coast of Baffin Island around Cape Walsingham. From there he headed south, passing the entrance to Cumberland Sound, which he had explored the previous year, without comment. Farther south, when the vessel was becalmed off the coast of Resolution Island, the men took the opportunity to see if they could catch some fish. These were so plentiful that they took 100 fine cod in half an hour. Then, when the wind picked up, they continued south through blustery weather. On 28 August, they anchored in a fine harbour, surrounded by wooded hills. Davis had sailed past the entrance to Hudson Strait in bad weather, and had thus failed to see it. By now, he was somewhere on the Labrador coast. He spent two days exploring the country around his anchorage, which he found well supplied with birds, particularly ptarmigan, and cod. When the weather cleared up, he continued south along the coast, anchoring, finally, in the mouth of a broad strait, probably Hamilton Inlet or the Strait of Belle Isle. He hoped to explore the strait, but the winds were contrary, forcing him to anchor in a convenient cluster of islands. While they were wind-bound, they took yet another fine catch of fish. This time, they decided to dry the fish on shore, leaving them there overnight, carefully covered to protect them from the elements. When the wind finally shifted to the northwest, on 6 September, Davis decided to head for home. First, however, he sent five of the sailors ashore to pick up the fish. But the natives were lying in ambush, and attacked them with a hail of arrows. Two of the sailors were killed on the spot, and two others were mortally wounded. The other one barely escaped by swimming out to the ship with an arrow sticking out of his arm. Davis scattered the natives with a couple of musket-shots, but by the time they had picked up the wounded men, the wind had risen to a full gale, forcing them to ride at anchor till the 11th. The return trip was apparently uneventful, for there were no further entries in the log till they arrived in the west country in early October.

Davis wrote to William Sanderson, his patron, on 14 October, presumably from his home in Sundridge. He outlined his own experiences, and suggested that if another expedition would be fielded the next summer, it could pay its own expenses through the profits that would derive from fur-trading and the cod-fishing. He pointed out that the *Sunneshine* had visited Gilbert Sound after exploring the East Greenland coast, and had returned from there with 500 seal-skins, and 140 half-skins and pieces. Davis's suggestion was so well received that planning was started immediately for a third trip to the northwest.

This third voyage was to be organized in a fundamentally different way from the first two. It was to be primarily a fishing expedition, designed to exploit the incredibly rich fishing grounds that Davis had discovered along the Labrador coast. In many ways this voyage is reminiscent of the Frobisher voyages of a decade earlier; in both instances, the search for a northwest passage, with its promise of an ultimate gain, was made subservient to the promise of immediate gain. The present plan, then, was as follows: the expedition would consist of three vessels that would sail in convoy to Gilbert Sound, but there they would separate. Davis himself would continue the search for the northwest passage in the *Ellin,* a pinnace owned by one of the London merchants; the other two vessels, the *Elizabeth* and the *Sunneshine,* would drop down to the Labrador coast where they would engage in the cod-fishery between 54° and 55° north. When he had completed his explorations, Davis was to join the vessels on the fishing grounds. It was believed that the trade in skins at Gilbert Sound, and the haul of fish on the Labrador, would more than defray the costs of the entire project.

Scattered throughout the records of the third voyage are a number of references to the type of trade goods that the English were carrying. Metal objects, as is understandable, were the most valuable items in the eyes of the Eskimo. In addition to iron knives, nails, pins and needles, however, they also accepted bracelets, bells, mirrors and glass beads with almost equal enthusiasm. One of the peculiarities of this trade, and indeed of most of the early trade throughout the north, was that both the Eskimo and the English thought they were driving a hard bargain. For the Eskimo were receiving priceless pieces of iron for superfluous skins; the Europeans, on the other hand, were receiving very valuable skins in exchange for baubles. It was a totally satisfactory arrangement for all

## John Davis, 1587

THE THREE VESSELS SAILED FROM DARTMOUTH on 19 May, with Davis himself aboard the *Elizabeth*. From the beginning, it proved to be an uncomfortable crossing. First, the *Ellen* broke her tiller, a mishap that held them up until repairs could be made. Six days later, the *Sunneshine* began to leak so badly that the fleet had to 'heave to' so more repairs could be made. Finding the leak was no easy task, for it meant shifting the cargo around so that the inside of the hull could be examined, a few feet at a time, till the leak was located. Only then could repairs be made. And no sooner was the *Sunneshine* pumped dry than the foremast of the *Ellin* was blown overboard in a gale. Again they 'hove to' for repairs. By that time, however, the wind had dropped off, and they discovered that the pinnace required at least a small gale to push her along at any reasonable speed. She was so slow in light airs that she had to be towed part way across the Atlantic by one of the barks. But such problems were fairly routine for Elizabethan seamen; they consoled themselves with the hope that 'a hard beginning would make a good ending.'

In spite of all their problems, the vessels dropped their anchors in Gilbert Sound exactly four weeks out of Dartmouth.

The next day, while the merchants began trading with the Eskimo, the carpenters started setting up a small pinnace they had carried from England in frame. This task, as usual, was carried out on a neighbouring island. And again as usual, parties were sent out in the ships' small boats to explore the surrounding countryside. One of the parties captured an Eskimo that day, 'a very strong lustie fellow.' Davis and the merchants may have wanted a captive to train as an interpreter, a widespread custom at the time. At a later period, incidentally, fur-traders would often leave one of their own young men with a native group so that he could learn the native language, and thus facilitate trade. On the other hand, Davis may have captured the young Eskimo to take home as nothing more than a curiosity.

The Eskimo community probably saw the matter in a totally different light. History has not recorded their view of the matter, however. All that we know is that the following night, about 2 A.M., the natives tore the two upper strakes from the pinnace that was being assembled on the island. When the English saw what was happening ashore, they started shooting at them. The natives then turned the pinnace on its side so they could use it as a shield against the hail of arrows. Seeing that their arrows were ineffective, Davis ordered one of the gunners to dislodge them with a cannon-ball. But for some reason, the gunner merely fired off a blank charge. The noise scared off the natives, who fled in their kayaks to another island where they removed the nails from the planks, then retreated deeper into the sound. Davis and his officers were astonished at the turn of events. They were expecting that 'the Savages that were hurt should run away without legs, (but) at length we could perceive never a man hurt, but all having their legges could carrie away their bodies.'

Davis had apparently planned on taking the small pinnace with him on his exploration; but without her two upper strakes, she was no longer suitable for that purpose. He decided, therefore, to hoist her aboard the *Elizabeth*, to assist with the fishing on the Labrador coast. Then, with everything in order, the vessels sailed from Gilbert Sound on 21 June. As soon as they had cleared the mouth of the sound, the *Elizabeth* and the *Sunneshine* headed southwest for Labrador, while Davis, in the *Ellin*, followed the coast of Greenland to the north. He paused from time to time to trade with the natives, who came far out to sea in their kayaks, bringing birds, fresh meat and seal-skins. Nine days after leaving Gilbert Sound, Davis reached his highest latitude at 72°12' north. There, near the present settlement of Upernavik, he named a lofty headland 'Sanderson his Hope,' after his patron , William Sanderson. The distance between Gilbert Sound and Sanderson his Hope, incidentally, is 8°12', or 492 nautical miles.

Although the sea was still clear of ice as far as he could see to the north, head-winds stopped him at that point. He shaped his course to the west, therefore, and ran '40 leagues and better, without the sight of any land.' Two days later, however, he was stopped by the middle pack of Baffin Bay. He coasted that mighty barrier for seventeen days before he could work his way through the ice. When he finally did get through, he found himself off the mouth of Cumberland Sound, the same broad inlet he had discovered during his first voyage. He explored the north shore of the sound for some sixty leagues. As he did periodically, Davis measured the variation of the compass at that point, and found that it was 30° west. He then returned to Davis Strait, and shaped his course to the south, following the coast of Hall Peninsula. Farther south, he passed the entrance to Frobisher Bay—which he named Lumleis Inlet—and another 'great gulfe, the water whirling and roring, as it were the meeting of tides.' This, of course, was the entrance to Hudson Strait. Davis showed no interest in exploring either of the sounds he had passed. Even had he wanted to, it would have been impossible at the time, for the wind was out of the west, and the mouths of both straits were choked with ice. So he continued south till he picked up a promontory marking the mainland side of the 'great gulfe' he had just crossed. He named the promontory *Cape Chidley*, after John Chidley, an old friend from Devonshire.

Following the Labrador coast south from the cape, he reached the latitude of 50° north on 19 August. He stayed close inshore from there on, watching for the *Elizabeth* and the *Sunneshine*, who were supposed to be fishing in that area. When no trace of the vessels could be found—for they had departed long since—he shaped his course for England. 'And thus, after much variable weather and change of windes, we arrived the 15 of September in Dartmouth, Anno 1587, giving thanks to God for our safe arrivall.'

While they were still off the southern coast of Labrador, on 17 July, Davis made an intriguing entry in his log. He said that they met 'a Shippe at Sea, and, as farre as wee could judge, it was a Biscaine; wee thought she went a fishing for Whales, for in 52° or thereabouts, we saw very many' (Markham, 1880, p. 48). It is obvious from Davis's comments that he was not at all surprised at meeting another vessel on the Labrador coast; nor had he expressed any astonishment at the behaviour of the Greenland Eskimo. And yet it *is* astonishing that the natives would paddle far out to sea in their kayaks, and carry seal skins with them, unless they went out there to trade. And if they paddled out for that purpose, it can only have been because they had traded with other European vessels before that, and knew that seal skins could be trades for iron. This hypothesis is supported, too, by the fact that Frobisher found iron nails and an iron trivet in the Eskimo tent that he visited near Cape Farewell on his 1578 voyage.

Because the earliest recorded voyages to Baffin Island and Greenland—apart from those of the Vikings—were those of Martin Frobisher and John Davis, we tend to think that they discovered those coasts. So far as historians and cartographers are concerned, they *did* discover them, and are quite worthy of our respect and admiration. For they were both remarkable seamen and navigators, and they did bring those coasts to the attention of historians and map-makers. Yet it is virtually certain that fishermen, and possibly merchants, had been visiting Greenland and Labrador for at least a few generations. It has been estimated, for example, that by 1578, the year of Frobisher's third voyage, there were 150 French ships and 200 other ships fishing off the Newfoundland and Labrador coasts. And in addition, there were some 30 Biscayan whalers in the same area (Cooke & Holland, 1978, p. 23).

Davis returned from his third voyage to find that England was facing the threat of invasion. The Spaniards were assembling a huge fleet for the invasion, and the English were preparing their defences. Ships were suddenly at a premium. Few could be spared for arctic exploration, even had the merchants wanted to continue their search for a northwest passage. But the merchants, too, were preoccupied with the impending invasion. Although the Spanish Armada was defeated the following year, in 1588, another decade was to pass before the merchants were able to continue the search. John Barrow (1818, p. 164) summed up their position at that time as follows: 'The English,' he said, 'could not see with indifference a lucrative commerce carried on with the eastern world by the Spaniards and Portugueze without endeavouring to enjoy a participation thereof.' After their initial failure to locate a northwest passage, the English had attempted to enter the Oriental trade by the southwest passage around the Cape of Good Hope. As Barrow pointed out, however, their real aim was not to carry on a legitimate trade with the natives of the east, but to wax rich 'by the more cheap and expeditious mode of plundering the Portugueze.' Only when these attempts ended in disaster, did the English look once more to the northwest.

## George Weymouth, 1602

THIS TIME, IT WAS THE NEWLY FORMED East India Company that took up the challenge. At a meeting held in London on

7 August, 1601, it was decided that they would send an expedition to search for the northwest passage (Stevens, 1886, p. 183). After discussions with George Weymouth, an experienced seaman and navigator who was chosen to lead the expedition, it was agreed that two vessels would be the most suitable number for the task. The vessels they purchased for the voyage were the 70-ton *Discovery* and the 60-ton *Godspeed;* the ships carried a total complement of thirty-two men and boys, and were provisioned for eighteen months. The *Discovery,* incidentally, occupies a unique position in the history of arctic exploration. During a fifteen year period—1602 to 1616—that remarkable vessel carried six expeditions into the Canadian arctic (Christy, 1894, p. 201). And on two of them, it wintered in the north, once with Henry Hudson at the bottom of James Bay, and once with Thomas Button at the mouth of the Nelson River. Unfortunately, we know almost nothing about the *Discovery* herself. In all probability, she was originally Dutch (Stevens, 1886, p. 208), but even that could be questioned. She is described variously as a bark, a pinnace, and a 55-ton fly-boat. She would have carried the six sails that were characteristic of the period: two square sails on the mainmast, two more on the foremast, a triangular lateen sail on the mizzenmast, and a spritsail slung on a yard under the bowsprit. Weymouth refers to both the *Discovery* and the *Godspeed* as fly-boats, and complained that they would take on a lot of water in a heavy sea because neither one had a spar deck.

Weymouth sailed from Radcliffe on 2 May 1602. After an uneventful passage across the north Atlantic, he coasted Cape Farewell, at the southern tip of Greenland, on 18 June; ten days later, he was off the east coast of Resolution Island. From that point on, Weymouth's journal becomes increasingly murky. He seems to have spent most of his time dodging ice-floes, and being shrouded in dense fogs. We do know, however, that he reached a latitude of about 69° north. We know, further, that the crew of the *Discovery* conspired to lock Weymouth in his cabin, take over the ship, and sail her back to England.

Weymouth became aware of their plans somehow, and managed to avoid an open mutiny. But he apparently agreed that thėy would shape their course to the south. On the way south, he entered Frobisher Bay, Hudson Strait and Ungava Bay. He then followed the coast of Labrador southeast to the entrance to Hamilton Inlet, or thereabouts, but never once went ashore. From there, about 54° north, he set sail for England on 19 August. The two ships arrived at Dartmouth on 5 September 1602.

The cause of the mutiny was apparently the men's fear of spending a winter in the Arctic. It is impossible, at this distance, to evaluate their apprehensions. Weymouth may have intended to winter in the Arctic, although no such intention is evident in either his comments, as recorded in the log, or his behaviour. The minutes of the East India Company, on the other hand, state quite clearly that Weymouth was not to return to England in the fall. Specifically, he was instructed (Stevens, 1886, p. 212) that he must not: 'himselfe returne or voluntarily suffer any of his company to returne back againe unto or towarde the Coast of England for any lett or impediment whatsoever untill he and thay have bestowed one yeare at the least from the tyme of their departure hence in goinge foreward, seekinge, soundinge and attemptinge the performinge this intended viage.'

On their arrival back in England, the ship's officers were called before the general council of the East India Company to explain their sudden and unauthorized return. John Drew, maste of the *Godspeed*, reported that the ringleader of the aborted mutiny was the Reverend John Cartwright, who sailed aboard the *Discovery*. When John Lane, the mate on the *Godspeed*, also pointed to Cartwright as the ringleader, Weymouth was exonerated. The merchants had thought of sending Weymouth on a second expedition in search of the elusive passage, but financial problems with an East Indian voyage around the Cape of Good Hope stood in the way. In urgent need of ready cash, the East India Company decided to

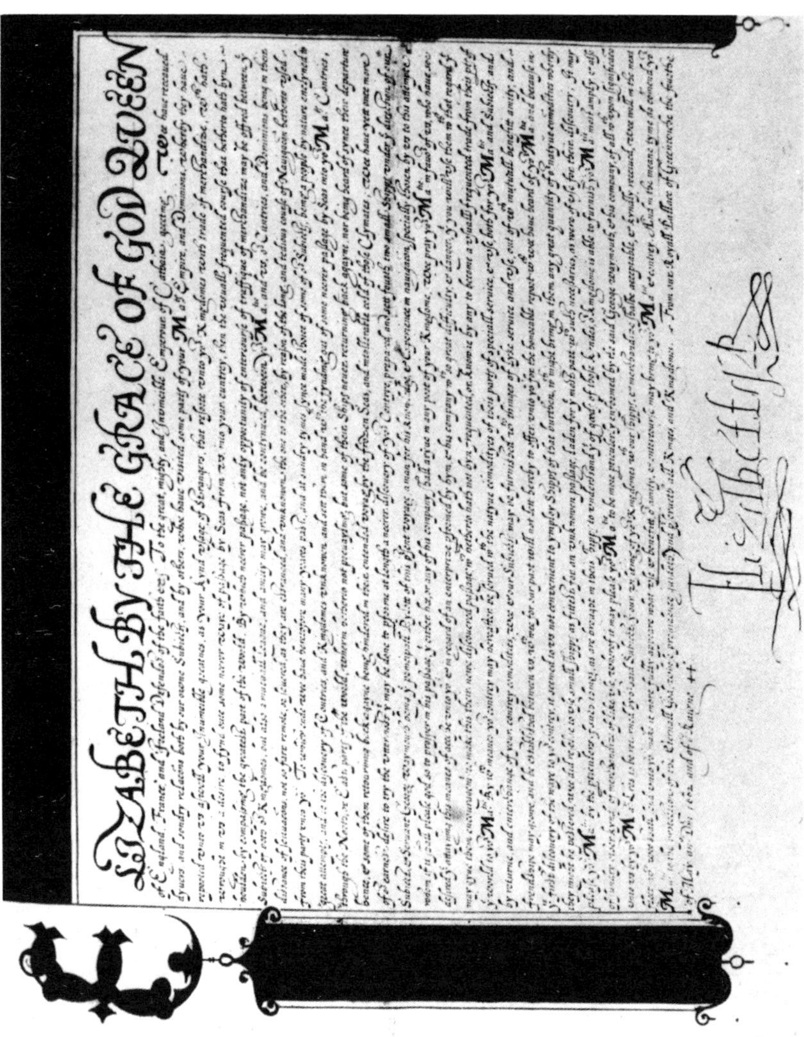

ELIZABETH BY THE GRACE OF GOD QUEEN

**Figure 6** The license, dated 4 May 1602, granted by Queen Elizabeth I to George Weymouth, captain of the Discovery and leader of the 1602 British Northwest Passage expedition sponsored by the East India Company. Lancashire Record Office, Lancaster.

abandon the search for a northwest passage, and to sell the *Godspeed* and *Discovery*. On 24 May 1603, they offered them for sale with all their furnishings at £300 each (Stevens, 1886, p. 242). It had not been a profitable summer.

## John Knight, 1606

THREE YEARS LATER, THE EAST INDIA COMPANY—with its financial problems apparently solved—decided to back another venture into the northwest. This time they shared the expense, and any profits that might accrue, with the Muscovy Company. A single vessel was provided on this occasion, the *Hopewell*, a 40-ton bark under Captain John Knight. Knight was an experienced arctic navigator, having sailed to Greenland the previous year on a Danish vessel.

He sailed from Gravesend on 18 April 1606. Eight days later he was anchored in St. Margaret's Sound in the Orkneys, where he was wind-bound for two weeks. His next landfall was on 13 May, when he picked up the Labrador coast near the present settlement of Hopedale. The crossing of the north Atlantic had been 'a long and tedious passage, destitute of any incident worth noticing' according to John Barrow (1818, p. 177). Just as they reached the coast, the tiny *Hopewell* was hit by a heavy gale out of the north. Knight managed to moor his ship before the storm reached its full intensity, But then the gale brought in vast fields of ice that were drifting south with the Labrador current. The ice tore off the ship's rudder, and nipped her so badly that she began filling with water. Knight finally managed to push her ashore in the bottom of a cove when she was on the point of sinking.

The next morning, on Thursday, 26 June, he set the men at unloading the ship, while he and six others went in search of a safe harbour where they might repair the damaged vessel. They rowed to a neighbouring island where Knight and three companions climbed to the top of a hill to survey the surrounding area. He left the other two men at the shore to guard the boat. The men at the shore became uneasy when the others failed to return after several hours had passed. They finally started sounding a trumpet and firing a musket, thinking that the others might have lost their way. They waited patiently for thirteen hours, but Knight and his companions never returned.

The rest of the party, meanwhile, had pitched a tent on shore, and had salvaged much of the food and clothing from the stricken *Hopewell;* and the carpenter had started assembling a small rowing-pinnace they had carried in frame. The next morning, a party of seven men was dispatched to the island where Knight and his companions had vanished. They went heavily armed because they feared that the missing men had either been captured by hostile natives, or eaten by some wild bests. By that time, however, the ice was so thick they could not even launch the boat.

That night, while the crew was asleep in the tent, two guards were posted on the beach, the bos'n and the steward. About 1:00 A.M. the next morning, while the steward was aboard the *Hopewell,* pumping out the bilges, the natives attacked without warning. The bos'n fired his musket, both to repel the attackers and to alert his shipmates. When the men emerged from the tent, and started firing their muskets, the natives withdrew. There had been eight natives and one dog in the attacking party. When it was all over, the natives were described as 'little people, tawney coloured, thick haired, little or no beard, flat nosed, and are man-eaters' (Christy, 1894, p. 111).

Afraid that the natives might attack them again, the men carried all their gear and provisions back aboard the *Hopewell* the next day, while two men stood guard on the beach. The carpenter, meanwhile, nailed the pinnace together, but had no time to do the caulking that would have made her watertight. They dragged the leaky pinnace over the ice to the *Hopewell,* then attacked the ice with picks and axes in an effort to free the ship. Then the wind apparently shifted, dispersing the ice, for they were able to row the disabled vessel out to sea on the night of 30 June. For two days they rowed their water-logged vessel through the ice pack, pumping constantly to deep her afloat. When the wind finally shifted to the north, they moored the *Hopewell* to a large ice-floe, and drifted rapidly south with the Labrador current. Although the men were exhausted with the constant rowing and exposure, they now set about hanging the rudder, which had been knocked adrift when they first went ashore. This, too, was a laborious task as new pintles and gudgeons—the hinges on which the rudder turns—had to be forged. And only when that was finished, could they turn their attention to stopping the more serious leaks in the vessel itself. Most of the leaks could be plugged up from the inside; but the major leak, near the front end of the keel, could not be reached from inside the hull because it was directly under some of the ship's timbers. To plug it from the outside, they smeared a wide strip of heavy canvas with a thick layer of tar and frayed rope, a mixture called 'oakum' then dragged the strip under the hull, and snugged it up tightly with ropes. This did not stop the leak, but it did reduce it to a manageable flow.

Following Knight's disappearance, the log of the voyage was kept by Oliver Brunel (or Brownel), a well-known Dutch navigator who was aboard the *Hopewell* in some unspecified capacity. Brunel now took charge of the battered vessel, and decided to sail her to Newfoundland for repairs before attempting the North Atlantic crossing to England. He raised the coast of Newfoundland on 21 July, near Fogo Island, where he met a fleet of twelve European fishing boats. The fishermen led him into Fogo Bay where they spent a month recaulking the *Hopewell,* and resting up from their ordeal. They arrived back in England on 24 September 1606.

## Henry Hudson, 1610-11

THE NEXT VOYAGE TO THE NORTHWEST, that of Henry Hudson in 1610, is one of the most widely known of all arctic expeditions, for it positively bristles with the stuff of drama. It was, first of all, a successful voyage in that it resulted in the discovery of a vast inland sea—a mediterranean, actually—that is still called Hudson Bay. It was also an exciting voyage, at least for the reader, because the seamen mutinied, and cast Hudson, his son John, and seven of the men adrift in a small boat, to disappear forever into swirling arctic mists. It also involves an intriguing mystery, for it turns out that large portions of the ship's log—from 3 August 1610 to 21 June 1611—are missing. It is strange indeed that the survivors were never called upon to explain this absence. The mutiny itself was glossed over by attributing it to the perfidy of men who had conveniently died on the return voyage. But throughout the drama, there is a thread of history that can still be followed.

It started, as usual, with a group of merchants and courtiers who had studied the journals of earlier voyages, the arguments of learned cosmographers, and the latest charts and globes of the cartographers. All the evidence, they believed, pointed to the existence of a northwest passage. And the rewards for actually finding such a passage would be so immense as to justify almost any expenditure. The primary figures behind Hudson's voyage were: Sir John Wolstenholme a wealthy merchant, and one of the founders of the East India Company; Sir Dudley Diggs, a diplomat and judge, as well as a stockholder in the East India Company; and Sir Thomas Smith, a wealthy London merchant who was the first governor of the East India Company. These men had set up a new corporate body for the venture, the Northwest Company. Henry Hudson, a well known arctic navigator, was chosen to lead the expedition. His instructions were to explore the inlets that Davis had seen leading westward from his strait. Although it is not mentioned in the records, it is highly probable that Hudson, as well as his backers, had backers, had decided to follow the path mapped out by Weymouth only eight years before. This suggestion is supported by a statement made by a later explorer, Luke Foxe, who says that it was Weymouth who lighted Hudson into his strait. In any event, Hudson was provided with Weymouth's old vessel, the *Discovery*, and provisions for only six months. In retrospect—and in view of what happened—Hudson's supplies seem totally inadequate. We must remember, however, that Hudson's was the ninth expedition that the merchants had sent in search for the passage; and none of the others had found it necessary or desirable to spend a winter in the northwest. In fact, the only party of western Europeans to have wintered in the Arctic prior to Hudson was the Willem Barentz expedition in search of a *northeast* passage. Barentz and his companions spent the winter of 1596-7 on the northeast corner of Nova Zemlya, an island northeast of the White Sea in Russia. The Northwest Company, as well as Hudson himself, had every reason, therefore, to believe that his supplies were adequate. If he were successful, he would spend the winter on some tropical island; and if he were unsuccessful, he would return to England in the fall, as the others had done.

Hudson sailed from London on 17 April 1610 (Asher, 1860, p. 93), with a crew of twenty-three, reaching Iceland three weeks later, after an uneventful passage. Head-winds kept him in Iceland until the end of May; only then was he able to set sail to the west. Picking up the coast of Greenland three days later, Hudson followed the coast to the south, rounded Cape Farewell, then shaped his course to the northwest. As is usual along that coast, he encountered vast fields of ice, but seems to have threaded his way through the pack without too much difficulty. Once he entered the inlet that both Davis and Weymouth had described, however, it was a different matter entirely. For Hudson Strait is something over 430 miles long, stretching from Cape Chidley in the east to Cape Wolstenholme in the west. Interminable fog-banks, particularly towards the western end of the strait, hang like a shroud across the narrow passage, while broad swaths of drifting ice are brought down from the northwest each summer by the current flowing out of Foxe Basin. Further hazards are presented by snow and freezing rain, as well as by glistening, grey icebergs, hard as granite, that wander in from Davis Strait.

It was 3 August when Hudson cleared the western end of the strait. It had been a hard passage, but a successful one so far as Hudson was concerned. As he gazed upon the broad waters stretching endlessly before him, he clearly thought that the elusive passage had been found. The merchants of England had devoted thirty-five years to the search; they had launched nine different expeditions to the northwest. And now the prize was theirs.

But the weather was still bad, and the men were apprehensive, so Hudson shaped his course to the south, in search of a warmer climate and more congenial surroundings. As he followed the coastline south, he thought he was following the western shore of the continent, or the back side of America, as it was called at the time. But he never did reach a warmer climate. Some 650 miles south of Cape Wolstenholme, he became trapped in a maze of shoals, reefs and islands at the bottom of what is now James Bay. There he was forced to spend the winter.

The precise location of Hudson's wintering-place is not known. We do know, however, that it was somewhere in the bottom of James Bay, and probably in the vicinity of Point Comfort. There, on 1 November 1610, they hauled their vessel ashore. And only nine days later they were solidly frozen in. They apparently spent the winter aboard the *Discovery*, although Philip Staffe, the carpenter, did build a small structure on shore. When they sailed from London, they had six month's provisions for the twenty-three people aboard (Asher, 1860, pp. 93 and 110). But they had already been at sea for six months before their arrival at the bottom of the bay; as a result they were already on short rations, even though they had killed and preserved a good quantity of water-fowl that they found nesting in incredible numbers at the western end of the strait. As soon as they were settled in their winter quarters, therefore, Hudson inventoried his remaining supplies, and offered to reward the men for any fish or meat they might contribute to the larder. Fortunately, they were in a rich area, for Abacuk Prickett, who kept a rough journal, comments as follows: '... for the space of three moneths wee had such store of fowle of one kinde (which were partridges as white as milke) that wee killed above an hundred dozen, besides others of sundry sorts; for all was fish that came to the net. The spring coming this fowle left us yet they were with us all the extreme cold. Then in their places came divers sort of other fowle, as swanne, geese, duck, and teale, but hard to come by' (Asher, 1860, p. 113). But these, too, finally drifted across the northern horizon, leaving a strangely quiet and empty land. 'Then,' Prickett continues, 'wee went into the woods, hilles, and valleyes, for all things that had any shew of substance in them, how vile soever.' Even 'the frogge (in his ingendring time as loathsome as a toade) was not spared.'

As soon as the ice went out of the bay, Hudson's men set a net, and on the first day caught 'five hundred fish, as big as good herrings, and some troutes.' But the fish, too, soon disappeared. Just before they left their wintering-place, a boat's crew fished for two and a half days, and brought back only 80 small fish, a catch which Prickett describes as 'a poore relieve for so many hungry bellies.'

It had been a hard winter. Scurvy had spread through the ship's company, but was apparently kept under reasonable control by the amount of fresh meat they were able to procure, mainly ptarmigan. They were assisted, too, by a concoction they brewed from the green and yellow leaves of a tree. This tree, we are told (Asher, 1860, p. 141) had leaves 'of an aromatical savour, and being boyled yeelded and oyley substance, which proved an excellent salve, and the decoction being drunke proved as wholesome a potion, whereby they were cured of the scorbute, sciaticas, croupes, convulsions, and other diseases,

**Figure 7** *The Last Voyage of Henry Hudson* (oil-on-canvas, 1881), by the Hon. John Collier (1850-1934). This nineteenth-century reconstruction depicts Hudson, his son Jack, and his loyal ship's carpenter, Philip Scarfe, aboard the shallop in which they, along with six scurvy-ridden sailors, were cast adrift in James Bay by the mutinous crew of the *Discovery* in the spring of 1611. The Tate Gallery, London.

which the coldnesse of the climate bred in them.'

Finally, on 12 June 1611, Hudson and his men sailed for home. But a mutiny that had been smouldering for months finally broke through to the surface when Henry Greene and part of the crew seized the vessel. Then, on the night of 23 June, while the *Discovery* was becalmed near what is now Charlton Island, Hudson, his son John, and six of the men were cast adrift in a small boat. After a thorough search of the vessel and a careful inventory of the seriously depleted stores, Greene appointed Robert Bylot as mate (a position which he had previously held), and shaped his course for Hudson Strait, where he hoped to lay in a supply of wild-fowl for the homeward voyage.

They reached the western end of the strait on 26 July. The following day, contrary winds made it impossible for them to reach the nesting-grounds where they had shot so many fowl the previous year. All they could do was send off the boat with a few of the men to scour the surrounding area.

The men found a 'good store of gulls, yet hard to come by, on the rocks and cliffes; but with their peeces they killed some thirtie, and towards night returned.' Two days later, Greene and his men met a band of Eskimo who were camped near the nesting-grounds. There was a brief but intense skirmish during which Henry Greene and two of his men were slain, as were at least two of the natives. However, the battered crew of the *Discovery* finally managed to kill and preserve some three hundred birds before shaping their course for England.

Robert Bylot, the new master of the vessel, put the men on short rations immediately, for all they had for the homeward voyage, apart from the wild-fowl they had just shot, was a small quantity of oatmeal. Each man's daily ration consisted of half a bird, and, while it lasted, a bit of the meal. And nothing was wasted. Even the bird-skins which had been tossed aside during more prosperous times were now eaten. After the feathers had been burned off, the skins were tossed into a pot where they became 'a great dish of meate, and as for the

thrown away.' Even the candles were finally eaten. Bennet, the cook, 'made a messe of meate of the bones of the fowle, frying them with candle grease till they were crispe, and, with vinegar put to them, made a good dish of meate.'

When they finally reached Beer Haven on the southwest coast of Ireland, they had to pawn their best anchor and cable before they could lay in fresh supplies of bread, meat, and beer. Hiring some local men to help them work the ship, the eight survivors then sailed to Gravesend in England. There, the crew was paid off, and Robert Bylot and Abacuk Prickett went up to London to report to Sir Thomas Smith. During the third week of October, 1611, the survivors, except for the ship's boy, Nicholas Syms, were examined by the master and wardens of Trinity House, London (Christy, 1894, p. 634). They concluded that Hudson had not reached the Pacific, which still lay far to the west, but had sailed into a broad bay. They also concluded, however, that the newly discovered bay was probably connected to the western sea by a passage that would be found somewhere to the northwest. This opinion was based on Hudson's report that there was a strong current flowing southeast from what is now Foxe Basin.

## Thomas Button, 1612-13

THE TRINITY HOUSE CONCLUSIONS were apparently accepted without reservation by Sir Thomas Smith and his colleagues in the Northwest Company, for they immediately set about organizing another expedition to follow up the exploratory work of Hudson. To lead the expedition, they selected Thomas Button, a former naval man. With two vessels, the *Resolution* and Hudson's old *Discovery*, Button sailed for the northwest on 14 April 1612. Because his journal has not survived, our knowledge of Button's exploration and wintering is extremely limited. What we do know is derived almost entirely from the summary that was presented by Luke Foxe in his book,

*Northwest Fox,* first published in London in 1635. We know, for example, that Abacuk Prickett and Robert Bylot were members of the crew, and we know that they were provisioned for 18 months. But the size of the crew is unknown. Button's instructions, however, have survived (Christy, 1894, pp. 636-641). Drawn up by Henry, Prince of Wales, on 5 April 1612, they admonished Button to permit no gambling, profanity, or blasphemy, and to hold daily religious services throughout the voyage. He was to pay particular attention to Sundays and holy days, which were to be 'christianlike observed with godlie meditacions.' He was to proceed first to Digges' Island, and from there was to stand over to the western main in the latitude of some 58°. There he was to anchor off some cape or headland, while he carefully measured the tidal stream. If the tidal flood streamed down from the north, then he was to search for the northwest passage in that direction; but if the rising waters of the tide flowed up from the south, then the passage, too, must lie to the south. This method of finding the northwest passage, or any similar passage, was standard procedure at the time. It was based on the fact that when the tide is rising in any bay or sound the water is flowing into that bay or sound from the larger body of water to which it is attached. Button, then, was to follow the tide which would—at least in theory—lead him through the northwest passage and into the larger body of water in the west, that is, into the fabled Pacific.

Button raised the western shore of Hudson Bay around 61°40' north, or about 175 miles north of the present town of Churchill, Manitoba (Christy, 1894, p. 165). From there he worked his way slowly down the coast until he reached the mouth of a river where he anchored about the middle of August. And there he wintered. He named the river the Nelson, after Robert Nelson, master of the *Resolution,* who died and was buried there. To protect them from floods and drifting ice, the vessels were drawn in close to the bank of the river, and shielded behind barricades of timber and earth.

Figure 8 Portrait of the Welsh explorer, Admiral Sir Thomas Button (?-1634), in court attire, his left hand resting on a globe to indicate the Arctic shores he charted during his 1612 expedition in search of the Northwest Passage. Private collection, Wales.

Living aboard one of the vessels, the men kept three fires burning all winter; and were well supplied, fortunately, with ptarmigan and other fowl, which they killed in incredible numbers. They also killed many wolves and bears, as well as three deer, probably caribou, that they found swimming across the river. Yet many of the crew perished during that long, hard winter. We are given no clue as to the number of men who died, nor are we told the cause of their death. We know only that the mortality rate was extremely high. But we can assume, with reasonable assurance, that they died of trichinosis and scurvy.

Although the ice broke up on the Nelson River on 21 April, it was another two months before the bay was reasonably clear of ice. Only then could Button move northward with his decimated crew, to continue his search for a passage that would lead to the Pacific. By late July he had worked his way into the passage, which was later named Sir Thomas Roe's Welcome, on the western side of Southampton Island.

Believing that he was embayed, he swung around to the south, then headed east toward Hudson Strait, and so to England. Although he had been unsuccessful in his search for the northwest passage, Button was convinced that such a passage did exist. He was convinced, further, that it would be found if a more thorough search of the northwest reaches of Hudson Bay were undertaken. For Button's discoveries had proved that the Master and Wardens of Trinity House were correct in their appraisal of the discoveries that Hudson had made. The Pacific still lay far to the west, far beyond the land that Button had discovered and named 'New Wales.'

## William Gibbons, 1614

ALL THAT WE KNOW ABOUT THE HAPLESS VOYAGE of Gibbons is a brief note in *Northwest Fox* (Christy, 1894, pp. 201-2), and a few editorial comments by Christy himself. Neither the date when Gibbons sailed from England, nor the date of his return is known; nor do we know the size of his crew. We *are* told, however, that the Gibbons expedition into the northwest was funded jointly by the Northwest Company and the East India Company (Christy, 1894, pp. 201-2), and that he sailed in the stalwart old *Discovery*, now on her fourth arctic voyage, with provisions for '12 Monethes.'

Foxe devotes but a single paragraph to Gibbons, a paragraph that reads as follows:

> Little is to be writ to any purpose, for that hee was put by the mouth of *Fretum Hudson*, and with the ice driven into a bay called by his companions Gibbons his Hole, in latitude about 57° upon the N.E. part of Stinenis, where he laid twenty weekes fast amongst the ice, in danger to have been spoyled, or never to have got away, so as the time being lost, he was inforced to returne.

## Robert Bylot and William Baffin, 1615

THE FAILURE OF GIBBONS NOTWITHSTANDING, the Northwest Company refitted the indomitable *Discovery* in 1615, and sent her on her third and final voyage into Hudson Bay (Markham, 1881). With Robert Bylot as master, and William Baffin as pilot, the small vessel dropped down the Thames on 18 April with a crew of twelve men and two boys. By 6 May she was off the coast of Greenland, feeling her way cautiously through the heavy stream of arctic ice that sweeps down through Denmark Strait, between Iceland and Greenland. Bylot slowly conned his vessel southward around Cape Farewell at the southern tip of Greenland, then moved northward into Davis Strait But the strait, too, was so choked with ice, and the weather was so bad, that he did not raise the entrance to Hudson Strait until 31 May. The following day, after snowing all morning, it finally cleared up. Then, when a northwest wind opened a narrow channel through the ice, Bylot worked the *Discovery* into a snug harbour on the southwest corner of Resolution Island and dropped her anchor.

Following the north shore of Hudson Strait, Bylot moved steadily westward, plotting his position so carefully that his course can still be followed today. But it was such a slow process—what with contrary winds, unpredictable currents and eddies, fog and drifting ice—that he did not raise Salisbury Island at the western end of the strait until 29 June. From there he moved northwest into what is now Foxe Basin, examining and checking the north and east coast of Southampton Island. But the entire area was packed with drifting ice, the tides were uncertain, and the weather was so bad that Bylot saw little hope of ever finding a passage through these alien seas. So he shaped his course for England. He passed Resolution Island on 5 August, and on 7 September was riding quietly at anchor in Plymouth Sound.

## Bylot and Baffin, 1616

THE NORTHWEST COMPANY WAS FINALLY convinced that the passage must lie far to the north, perhaps through the strait that John Davis had discovered in 1585. To investigate that possibility, they fitted out the *Discovery* with a compliment of 12 men and two boys for yet another voyage into the Arctic. Bylot and Baffin, her old master and pilot, sailed from Gravesend on 26 March 1615, and again shaped their course for the northwest. In Davis Strait they passed Hope Sanderson, Davis' farthest north, and continued on for another three hundred miles.

They finally reached a latitude of 77°45' north, a record that was to stand for 236 years. During the summer, they mapped the entire shoreline of Baffin Bay, noting Smith Sound, Jones Sound, and Lancaster Sound. The latter, as it turned out, was not a sound. Although they failed to recognize it as such, it was in fact the long sought entrance to the northwest passage. On

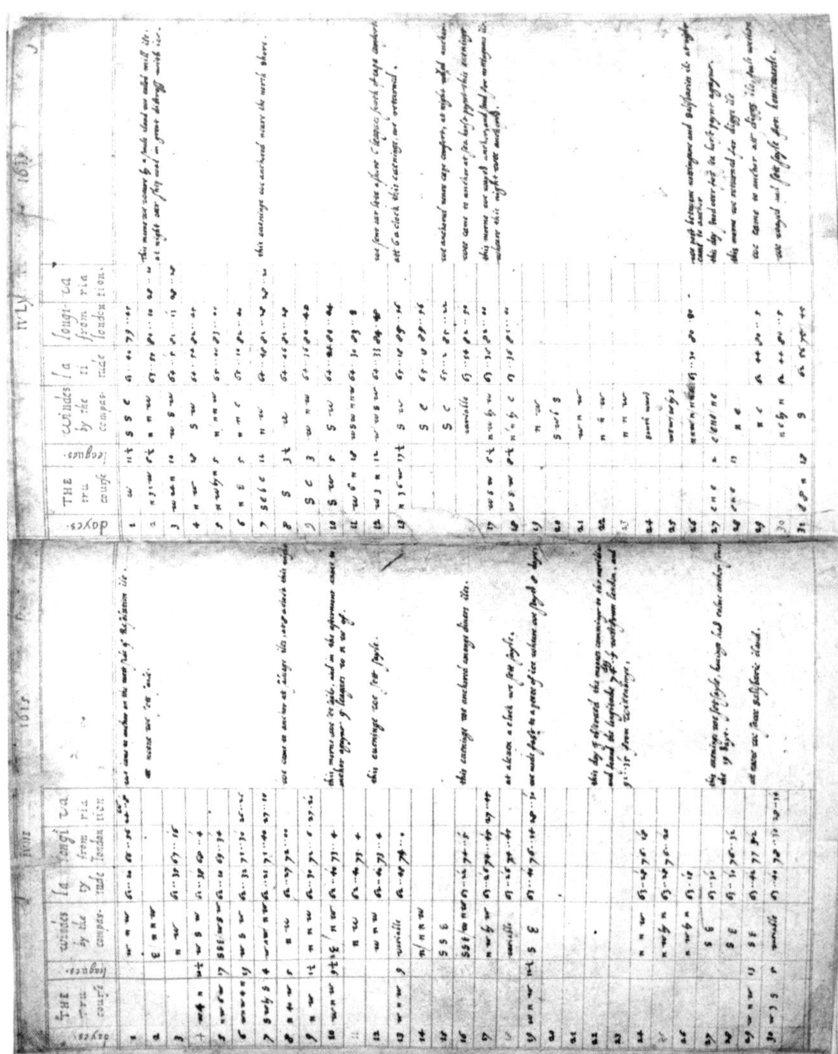

**Figure 9** Two pages from the manuscript log of William Baffin (1584?-1622) for his voyage in search of the Northwest Passage, recording observations made in June and July 1615. British Library, London.

his return to England, Baffin wrote to Sir John Wolstenholme to say that '... there is no passage nor hope of passage in the north of Davis Straights. We having coasted all, or neere all the circumference thereof, and finde it to be no other than a great bay, as the voyage doth truely shew' (Markham, 1881, p. 150).

## William Hawkridge, 1619

HAWKRIDGE'S VOYAGE, LIKE THAT OF GIBBONS, is known to us only through the brief note recorded in Foxe (Christy, 1894, pp. 248-59). Rundall, however, found some references to the voyage in the records of the East India Company (Rundall: 1849, pp. 150-51); these tell us that the voyage was undertaken when Sir John Wolstenholme proposed 'an intended triall to be made once againe in discovering the Norwest passage.' Sir John was assisted in the venture by some of his friends, as well as by the East India Company. We have no data whatever on the ship or ships that were employed, or the size of the crew. We do know, however, that Hawkridge, like Gibbons, had sailed with Thomas Button in 1611-12, and was therefore an experienced arctic pilot. But his log, while bristling with information on latitudes, distances, soundings and similar nautical details, is totally worthless, for it is impossible to follow his track on a nautical chart.

Christy sums up the Hawkridge voyage with the following comments (1894, p. 149fn.). 'The only thing the narrative does make clear is that, wherever he went, he cruised about in an apparently aimless way, first in one direction then in another, and that he frequently crossed over his own track.'

## Jens Munk, 1619-20

WHEN THE ENGLISH MERCHANTS SHIFTED their attention to Davis Strait on the higher northern latitudes, in 1616, Hudson

Bay again faded into limbo. The English no longer had any reason to visit that ice-encrusted mediterranean, for they had seen it only as a passage. When it failed to live up to its early promise, it was abandoned. It simply had no intrinsic value. While the English had been exploring the bay, however, their comings and goings were watched with considerable interest—and possibly envy—by King Christian IV of Denmark and Norway. That monarch had taken an active personal interest in the expansion of Danish trade and industry, particularly in the whale-fishery in Spitzbergen, far to the north of Lapland. And like the Dutch, the French and the English, he was anxious to share in the incredible wealth that was being generated by the trade in Oriental spices.

He decided, therefore, to undertake his own search for the northwest passage. To head the expedition, he appointed Captain Jens Munk, probably the best known and most able seaman in the Danish navy. With two vessels, the *Unicorn* and the *Lamprey*, Munk sailed from Copenhagen on 9 May 1619, with a crew of 64 men—48 in the *Unicorn and* 16 in the *Lamprey* (Gosch, 1897). Shaping his coursed to the northwest, he passed between the Orkney and Shetland Islands, and continued on until he sighted the Faeroes. From there he angled off to the west until he raided the coast of Greenland at 61°25' north on 20 June. As usual, the coast was bristling with ice which forced him to stand off at least 20 miles. But he worked his way to the south, passed Cape Farewell on the 30th, then headed northwest into Davis Strait. This, too, was packed with ice, however, and before Munk was able to reach the western end of Hudson Strait, he had mistakenly sailed into both Frobisher Bay and Ungava Bay. But he finally arrived at Digges Island, then continued on to Mansel Island. Because the instructions that the court had given him have not survived, we have no clue as to his plans. We know only that he sailed from Mansel Island in a southwesterly direction until he picked up a low, wooded shore on 7 September 1619. And there, in the mouth of what is now the Churchill River, he settled down to spend the winter.

Working his ships across the rock-strewn tidal flats, he moored them as closely as possible to the western edge of the river, than banked them up with wood, earth and stones to protect them from drifting ice. Taking the heavy brass cannon from the upper decks, he stowed them in the holds. Next he built three large fireplaces aboard the *Unicorn*, two on the deck and one in the steerage, so that each of the men would have a place to warm himself, and dry his clothing. A small building on shore completed his arrangements for the wintering.

When they had settled in, Munk must have been well pleased with his situation. The vessels were sound, the men were healthy, and food and drink were plentiful. He had a surgeon aboard to see to the physical well-being of the men, and a priest to keep them spiritually vigorous. And at 50°47' north, his winter harbour was 97 miles farther south then Bergen, Norway. As the entire Norwegian coast is ice-free all winter, even as far north as Lapland, he was not at all worried about the weather, even though it was deteriorating rapidly. What he did not know, of course, was that the entire Scandinavian coast was warmed by the gentle currents of the gulf stream; at Churchill, on the other hand, he was exposed to the raw fury of an arctic winter.

During the fall and early winter the men spent much of their time ashore, hunting ptarmigan, and trapping small game. Munk encouraged them in these pursuits as it kept them active, and also provided the party with the occasional bit of fresh meat. But dropping temperatures and deeply drifting snow finally made hunting impossible. Confined to the ship, the men could do nothing but huddle around the fires. They remained healthy, however until the beginning of the new year, when a strange and fatal malady spread rapidly throughout the crews. The men had scurvy, which they recognized, but were also suffering from some additional and terrifying ailment which they could not identify: 'It was a peculiar malady,' Munk wrote in January, 'in which the sick

**Figure 10** A woodcut from the account of his 1619-1620 voyage by Jens Ericksen Munk (1579-1628), captain of the Enhiöningen, conflating two occasions when the crew disembarked on the south shore of Baffin Island, near Jackman Sound in 68°E. In the upper left, sailors are depicted being welcomed by a group of Inuit; below, at another anchorage, a hunting party shoots a caribou, mistakenly identified as a reindeer, after which Munk named nearby 'Ren Sound' (Reindeer Channel). From *The Expedition of Captain Jens Munk to Hudson's Bay in Search of a North-west Passage in 1619-20,* ed. by C.C.A. Gosch (London: The Hakluyt Society, 1897). Courtesy The Hakluyt Society, London.

men were usually attacked by dysentery about three weeks before they died' (Kenyon, 1980, p. 26).

By the third week in May, most of the crew had perished, while the few survivors were lying helplessly in their bunks. The bodies of the men who had died earlier had all been buried with at least a semblance of Christian ritual, but that was no longer possible. Now the bodies 'were simply left in the steerage, for there was no one left who had the strength to bury them, or even to throw them overboard.' Elaborating on his earlier comment, Munk then described their malady as follows:

> The illness that had fallen upon us was rare and extraordinary, with most peculiar symptoms. The limbs and joints were miserably joined together, and there were great pains in the loins as though a thousand knives had been thrust there. At the same time the body was discoloured as when someone has a black eye, and all their limbs were powerless. The mouth, too, was in a miserable condition, as all the teeth were loose, so that it was impossible to eat (Kenyon, 1980, p. 34).

This strange catalogue of infirmities contains some of the well known symptoms of scurvy: but it probably contains symptoms of trichinosis as well. In any event, half of the crew was dead by March, 1620, and by 4 June, only Munk and two of the men were left alive. In spite of their weakened condition, however, the three survivors of that terrible winter managed to work the small sloop, the *Lamprey*, back to Norway, where they dropped their anchor on 21 September 1620. It had not been a prosperous voyage.

## Luke Foxe, 1631

THE ENGLISH, MEANWHILE, REMINDED themselves from time to time that there was still a portion of Hudson Bay that had not been explored. For no European had ever seen that stretch of coastline to the east of Button's wintering-place at the mouth of the Nelson River. Hudson had mapped the bay where he had wintered far to the southeast, but what lay in between those two known points? And even the parts of the bay that had been visited had not been thoroughly explored. There was a distinct possibility, then, that a northwest passage might yet be found if the shores of that vast inland sea were examined more thoroughly.

Philosophers and cosmographers had been arguing for generations about whether or not a northwest passage did in fact exist; and generations of merchants had calculated to the nearest farthing the profits that such a passage would surely provide. The discovery of new lands and trade routes was also of interest to the king and court, for such exploits bathed the crown in reflected glory, and also made substantial contributions to the royal coffers. And so, in 1629, when Luke Foxe, a master mariner of Hull, petitioned the court for assistance with yet another voyage to the northwest, King Charles I agreed to provide him with a vessel.

Foxe selected the *Charles*, a vessel of some 70 or 80 tons, and signed on a crew of 20 men and two boys. With the assistance of the London adventurers he provisioned her for 18 months, then dropped down the Thames from London on 5 May 1631. Because the discoverers of the northwest passage would be granted a monopoly of the very lucrative trade through that waterway, there was an intense commercial rivalry between the merchants of the different seaports at the time. The merchants of Bristol therefore, decided that they, too, would send an expedition in search of the northwest passage. First, they approached the court, suggesting that the two groups of merchants, those of London and Bristol, should share in the rights and privileges that would result from any important discovery. When King Charles agreed, the Bristol Society of Merchant Venturers prepared the 70-ton *Henrietta Maria*, named after England's queen, for a voyage of 18 months. Captain Thomas James, a native of Bristol, was placed in command of the vessel, which, similar to Foxe's *Charles*, had a crew of 22 men and boys. James set sail from Bristol on 3 May 1631, five days after Foxe had sailed from London.

The journal that Foxe published in 1635 carries the following warning:

> ... Gentle reader, expect not heere any florishing Phrases or Eloquent Tearmes; for this Child of mine, begot in the Northwest's cold Clime (where they breed no Schollers) is not able to digest the sweet milke of Rethorick that's food for them (Christy, 1894, pp. 261-407).

This was a timely warning, for Foxe, whose formal education was apparently quite limited, presents us with some rather pedantic and convoluted prose. This does not obscure the fact, however, that he was an excellent seaman, an exceptionally well-trained navigator, and an astute observer. He was, for example, one of the first navigators to use logarithms in his computations, a skill he had learned from his patron, Henry Briggs, the mathematician.

Leaving the Thames, Foxe sailed north along the east coast of England to the Orkneys, before shaping his course for the new world. He apparently stayed south of the usual track, for he failed to pick up the east coast of Greenland, although he did encounter a bit of the usual ice when he was off Cape Farewell. The first land he raised, on 20 May, was the North Foreland at the entrance to Frobisher Bay. As usual, the bay was packed with drifting ice, but Foxe managed to work his way south to Resolution Island, where he turned west into Hudson Strait.

After coasting the north shore of the strait, he sailed south of Nottingham and Coats Islands, then headed northwest into the channel between Southampton Island and the mainland to the west. Foxe recognized this as the same channel that Thomas Button had explored 18 years earlier. On 27 July, at 64°10' north, Foxe discovered an island that he named Sir Thomas Rowe's Welcome, and that he described as follows:

> ... The Island was a Sepulchre, for that the Salvages had laid their dead

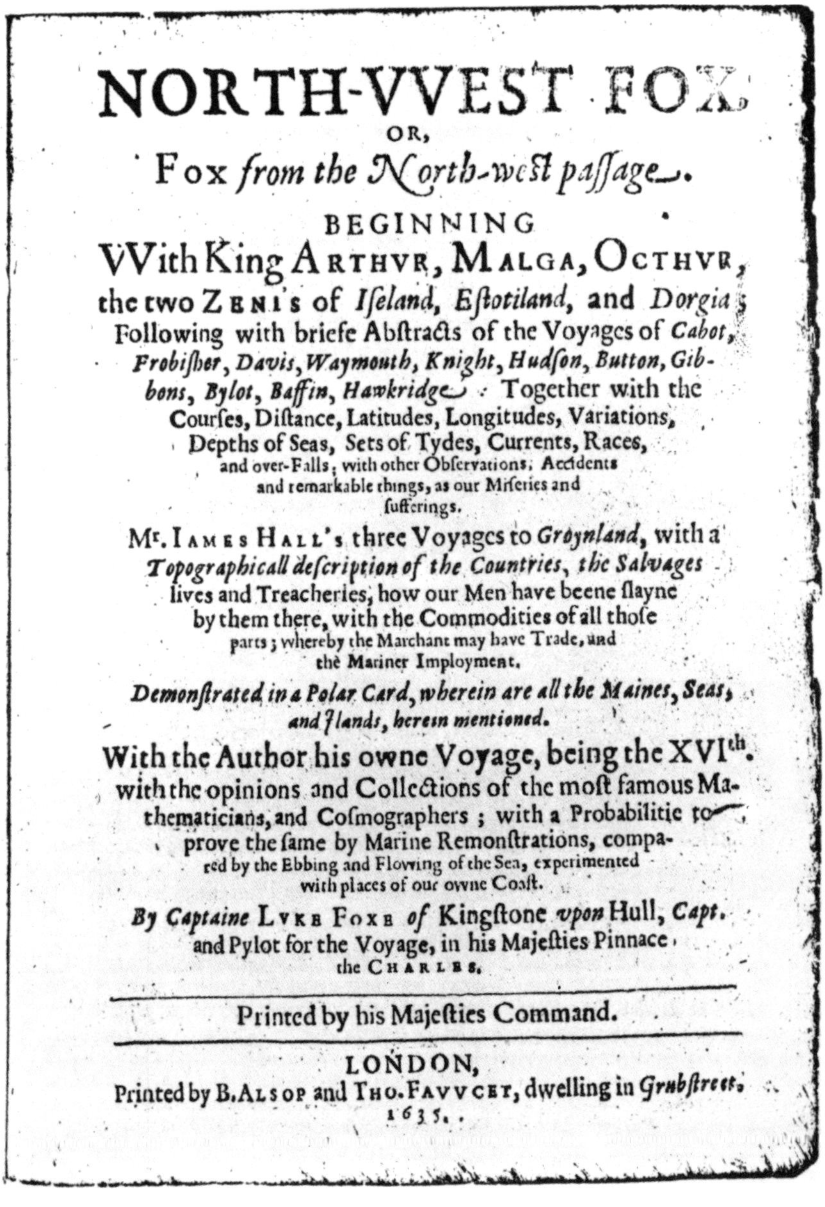

NORTH-VVEST FOX,
OR,
Fox *from the North-west passage*.
BEGINNING
VVith King ARTHVR, MALGA, OCTHVR,
the two ZENI's of *Iseland, Estotiland*, and *Dorgia*;
Following with briefe Abstracts of the Voyages of *Cabot, Frobisher, Davis, Waymouth, Knight, Hudson, Button, Gibbons, Bylot, Baffin, Hawkridge*: Together with the Courses, Distance, Latitudes, Longitudes, Variations, Depths of Seas, Sets of Tydes, Currents, Races, and over-Falls; with other Observations, Accidents and remarkable things, as our Miseries and sufferings.
Mr. IAMES HALL's three Voyages to *Groynland*, with a *Topographicall description of the Countries, the Salvages* lives and Treacheries, how our Men have beene slayne by them there, with the Commodities of all those parts; whereby the Marchant may have Trade, and the Mariner Imployment.
*Demonstrated in a Polar Card, wherein are all the Maines, Seas, and Ilands, herein mentioned.*
With the Author his owne Voyage, being the XVI[th].
with the opinions and Collections of the most famous Mathematicians, and Cosmographers; with a Probabilitie to prove the same by Marine Remonstrations, compared by the Ebbing and Flowing of the Sea, experimented with places of our owne Coast.
*By Captaine* LVKE FOXE *of* Kingstone *vpon* Hull, *Capt.* and Pylot for the Voyage, in his Majesties Pinnace the CHARLES.

Printed by his Majesties Command.

LONDON,
Printed by B. ALSOP and THO. FAVVCET, dwelling in *Grubstreet*. 1635.

**Figure 11** Title-page of *North-West Fox, or, Fox from the North-west passage* (London, 1635), by Luke Foxe (1586-1636), recounting his 1631 expedition in search of the Northwest Passage, during which he met Thomas James while exploring the south-western shore of Hudson Bay. Metropolitan Toronto Library.

(I cannot say interred), for it was all stone, as they cannot die therein, but lay the Corpses upon the stone, and wall them about with the same, coffining them also by laying the sides of old sleddes above... (Christy, 1894, p. 319).

From there, Foxe shaped his course to the south, following the coast, and searching for a passage that might lead to the west. Although he reported that he was 'never without sight of land,' he failed to notice the broad entrance to Chesterfield Inlet. By 8 August he was anchored off the shoals at the mouth of the Nelson River. He spent the next two days working his way slowly into the shoal and rock-strewn mouth of the river. Foxe, at the time, was looking for a convenient spot to assemble a prefabricated pinnace that he had brought with him from England. He was also anxious to find a suitable piece of timber that he could fashion into a new main yard for the *Charles*, the old one having been damaged.

Foxe finally found a likely spot on the north or right bank of the river and dropped his anchor in five fathoms:

The ship being moored [he says,] I went on land and found the Vallie very convenient to set up a tent and to build the Pinnace in; and here wee found some store of Hogsheads and Pipestaves which had been yron-bound, one main top, a top-gallant mast, diverse blocks, and the sides of staved chests, and diverse reliques of some *English* Vessel, which I tooke to have perished, or been left, not farre from hence. And indeed I did assure my selfe it must be that of *Sir Thomas Button;* but as yet I have not found a tree will make a Mayne yard' (Christy, 1894, pp. 342-43).

A few days later, while most of the men were helping the carpenter set up the pinnace, Foxe sent the surgeon—or Chirurgen, as he called him—with Samuel Blades, one of the men, to search for a tree large enough to fashion into a main yard. When they returned from searching the river ban to the east of their camp, they reported that all the trees in the area were too small. However, they also reported that

> by a little creeke about a mile off, they had found on shoare certaine broken anchors and cable rope, with other small ropes, also one broken Gun, with many round and crosse-barre shot of lead and yron, one Grapnel, and store of firewood piled up, with one tent covered with old sailes, and a Crosse, which had been set up, but was puled or fallen down, with the inscription rased out (Christy, 1894, p. 344).

These, of course, were additional relics of Button's wintering.

By the 18th, with the pinnace completed and stowed on the deck of the *Charles*, and with a two-week's supply of fire-wood aboard, they were ready to leave. First, however, they raided the fallen cross they had found, and nailed to it a sheet of lead bearing the following inscription:

> I suppose this Crosse was first erected by Sir Thomas Button, 1613. It was againe raised by Luke Foxe, Capt. of the *Charles*, in the right and possession of my dread Soveraigne Charles the first, King of Great Brittaine, France and Ireland, Defender of the Faith, the 15 of August, 1631 (Christy, 1894, p. 348).

Held up by adverse winds, Foxe was not able to clear the river-mouth until 20 August, when he continued examining the unexplored coastline stretching away to the southeast. Nine days later, near the mouth of the Winisk River, he met Captain Thomas James in the *Henrietta Maria* of Bristol. The two explorers dined together aboard James' vessel, then went their separate ways. Foxe continued eastward to what is now Cape Henrietta Maria at the top of James Bay.

From there, he sailed almost due north until he raised the coast of Coats Island; then, shaping his course to the northwest, he sailed into what is now Foxe Channel, and so into Foxe Basin. He was still looking for a strong tidal flood from the west or northwest, a flood that could only come from the western sea. But he could find no such flood. Finally, at 65°30' he made the following entry in his journals:

The weather had beene for about 3 weeks before, nothing but snowe, frost and sleet at best, our selves, ropes, and sayles froaze, the sun seldome to be seene, or once in five dayes, the nights 13 houres long, the moone wayning. And in conclusion, I was enforced either to seeke for harbour, or freeze to death in the sea (Christy, 1894, p. 412).

The nearest harbour, however, was at Port Nelson, and even if he could have reached that haven, there was the possibility that his provisions would not last through a long arctic winter. These considerations were reinforced, too, by the memory of the terrible mortality that the Hudson and Button expeditions had suffered during their winterings. On 12 September, therefore, he sailed for home.

## Thomas James, 1631-32

WHEN THOMAS JAMES MET FOXE off the mouth of the Winisk River on 29 August, he had already been in Hudson Bay for well over a month, having cleared Hudson Strait on 16 July. From there, he had sailed directly across the bay to Hubbarts Hope, at 59°40' north, where he arrived on 11 August. Following the coast to the south, he examined the shoreline and checked the tides, but failed to locate either a passage to the west or any other significant geographical feature. Until he was east of Port Nelson, of course, he was following a coastline that had already been explored by Thomas Button. James arrived at a cape that he named 'Henrietta Maria' on 3 September. Although their paths did not cross, Foxe arrived there on the same day.

James spent the next month—from 3 September to 3 October—in a vain attempt to work his way south to a more congenial climate. Actually, he was hoping to find a passage that would lead him to the river of Canada, that is, to the St.

**Figure 12** Engraved portrait of Captain Thomas James (c. 1593- c. 1635) at the age of forty, from *The Voyages of Captain Luke Foxe of Hull, and Captain Thomas James of Bristol In Search of a North-West Passage, 1631-32*, ed. by Miller Christy (London: The Hakluyt Society, 1894). Courtesy, The Hakluyt Society, London.

Lawrence. But he was trapped in a maze of small islands, reefs and shoal water, a maze of such complexity that it has not yet been properly charted. All hope of reaching a more temperate climate had to be abandoned when constant rain, fog and snow-squalls warned them that time was running out.

Realizing finally that he was trapped, James searched frantically for some protected bay or creek where he could winter his ship. But none could be found. Finally, after a heavy gale that lasted several days, James found himself in a shallow, reef-strewn bay. When the gale moderated on 3 September, he moved his vessel deeper into the bay, and dropped her anchor.

> Presently [he tells us] I went ashore to see what comfort I could find. That was the first time I put foot on that island, the island where we were destined to spend the winter. I noticed deer tracks and some fowl: but what excited me most was a break in the coastline that looked like the mouth of a river. We hurried over with great hopes but found the entrance to be solidly blocked by a sand-bar that was covered at high tide by only two feet of water. Yet inside the bar was a most excellent harbour with four fathom of water. In the evening, when I returned aboard, I had nothing but hopes with which to comfort our sick men (Kenyon, 1975, p. 57).

By that time, with the bay beginning to freeze over, and with many of the men weakened by exhaustion and scurvy, James realized that he could no longer move the vessel. All he could do was to lay out a heavy anchor, and winch her as close to shore as possible. Then he took in his sails—the very wings of his ship—and settled down for the winter. The crew, meanwhile, had built a small structure on shore, where the sick could be housed in relative comfort. By the 26th, the situation was so desperate that James decided to carry all his provisions ashore, then winch his vessel out into deeper water and sink her. He was fully aware of the risk he was taking, but felt that he had no choice. For by that time the ship was so heavily

**Figure 13** The *Susan Constant,* a modern replica of Thomas James's ship, the *Henrietta Maria,* in which he explored Hudson Bay and James Bay in 1631-32. Courtesy, Jamestown Foundation, Williamsburg, Virginia.

coated with ice that some of the ropes were as thick as a man's waist. And if a storm should descend upon them—as one surely would—the rising surf would pound the ship against the bottom with such violence that she would be destroyed. It was a hard choice, yet not without precedent; for James probably knew that in 1577, only 54 years earlier, Martin Frobisher had sunk a pinnace on Baffin Island 'minding to have him againe next year.'

Once the decision to sink her had been made, the men started ferrying their gear ashore. As the bay gradually filled up with drifting ice, James and his men prayed that it would freeze solid, and relieve them of the terrible extremity of sinking the only vessel that could carry them to safety. But it was not to be. On the 29th, when a gale from the northwest raised a heavy surf, the *Henrietta Maria* began pounding heavily and rhythmically against the bottom. In desperation, James and the carpenter descended into the bowels of the ship with a large auger and drilled a hole through her side. As the vessel filled with water, the pounding gradually subsided. By late afternoon she was bedded deep in the sand, with only her superstructure and naked spars rising above the waves.

The camp where James wintered consisted finally of three small buildings. Their dwelling house was a wattled structure, 20 feet square, covered with the mainsail from the ship. Apart from the gables, which rose to the ridge-pole, the walls were six feet high. A small hole was left at the top of each gable so that smoke from the central fire could escape. The inside of the house was lined with strips of canvas, and bunk beds were built against three of the walls. Their second structure was a cook-house and dining room slightly smaller than the first, but built in the same way. The third structure was a simple lean-to which they used as a store-house. Because of the danger of fire, the buildings were placed 20 feet apart. In honour of Charles, Prince of Wales, James named their lonely settlement 'Charles Town,' which they contracted to 'Charlton,' and the island, 'Charlton Island.'

As the snow rose higher and higher around the houses, it became increasingly difficult to trap the foxes that provided the men with an occasional bit of fresh meat. Even collecting dry wood for the fires became a problem. But their main problem throughout that long, hard winter was the piercing cold and scurvy. By February two thirds of the men were under the surgeon's care for scurvy and frostbite. 'Some,' James tells us, 'had sore mouths and loose teeth, and gums so swollen with rotten flesh that the surgeon had to cut it away daily.' And shortly after Christmas, 'many of the men were afflicted with such sore mouths that they could eat neither beef, pork, fish nor porridge. Their diet consists mainly of bread and oatmeal which they pounded into flour in a mortar then fried in a frying-pan with a little oil' (Kenyon, 1975, p. 93).

By 15 May, most of the snow was gone, and the ponds and small lakes were free of ice, but the bay itself was still solidly frozen. Not until the end of the month was there enough open water along the shore for them to reach the ship by boat. At that time, too, they found vetches growing along the shore. These they picked and fed to the sick men, with results that were virtually miraculous. Each day they picked more of the tender green shoots as they appeared through the sand. After they were washed and cooked,

> we ate them with oil and vinegar that had been frozen. It was an excellent and refreshing sustenance, and most of us ate nothing else. Sometimes we would crush them and mix the juice with our beverage; sometimes we ate them raw with our bread (Kenyon, 1975, p. 101).

On 22 May they went out to the vessel at low tide, manned the pumps, and pumped her completely dry. Then they plugged up the holes they had bored through the hull to sink her, so that she would rise with the incoming tide. After they removed the ballast to lighten the craft, they gradually winched her out into deeper water, and dropped the anchor. They spent the next month digging the ice out of the ship, bending on the sails and hauling their gear aboard. Then, on Monday, 2 July 1632, James wrote in his journal:

> We were up early, stowing our gear, putting things in order and weighing our anchors. When the last anchor was raised, we knelt in prayer, beseeching God to continue his mercies to us, and thanking him for having thus restored us. We found that the ship was sound; we still had plenty of the provisions which we had brought out from England and we were in fairly good health and getting stronger by the day. Thus we weighed anchor and came cheerfully to sail (Kenyon, 1975, p. 13).

When James arrived back in Bristol on 22 October 1632, he was convinced that there was no northwest passage below 66° north. And any passage lying in a higher latitude would be so remote, and so pestered with ice, that it would have no commercial value. The merchants of Bristol, and indeed all of England, apparently accepted James' verdict. The search for a northwest passage was abandoned.

## Maps

**Figure 14** A map by James Beare showing the direct route from Europe to the Orient by way of 'straightes' across the top of North America, published by Captain George Beste, Frobisher's lieutenant aboard the *Aid* on his second voyage and captain of the *Anne Frances* on the third, in *A True Discourse of the Late Voyages of Discoverie, for the Finding of a Passage to Cathaia* (London, 1578). Courtesy, The Hakluyt Society, London.

**Figure 15** The chart of Henry Hudson, first published by Henry Gerritsz in 1612, which adds Hudson's discoveries to those of Frobisher and Davis. 'Quine Elizabets Forlandt' is incorrectly placed on the southeast coast of 'Groelandia' (Greenland), an error originating with the first printed maps of Frobisher's voyages. National Map Collection, National Archives of Canada (Map H12/1102-1612).

**Figure 16** *Autograph Map of Baffin's Fourth Voyage to the North West* in 1615, indicating the explorer's route into Hudson Strait and the mouth of Foxe Basin. Original from Baffin's manuscript log in the British Museum, reproduced in facsimile in his *Voyages,* edited by Sir Clements Markham (London: Hakluyt Society, 1888). Courtesy, The Hakluyt Society, London.

**Figure 17** *The Plan of Sayling for the discovery of a Passage into the South Sea, 1631, 1632.* Engraving from *The Dangerous Voyage of Capt. Thomas James,* second ed. (London: Payne, 1740; first ed., 1633). Royal Ontario Museum, Canadian Decorative Arts Department, Toronto.

**Figure 18** Map of the Arctic regions by the Dutch cartographer William Janszon Blaeu (1571-1638), c. 1635. Metropolitan Toronto Library.

EAST
NORTH
Polus Arcticus
SOVTH
WEST
TERRA. SEPTEN=TRIONA=LIS.
TERRA AVSTRALIS.
ASIA
EVROPA
AFRICA
AMERICA
Frobushers Straightes
Circulus Articus
tropicus cancri
Circulus æquinoctialis
tropicus capricorni
Circulus Antarticus
Mare atlantica
Mare Pacificum.
Mar del zur.
Oceanus Australis
cabo de buona speranza
Peru
Magellanes
terra del fuego
Red sea
Arabia
India
mare caspium
tartaria
nilus
montes lunæ
Canada
Bay of myxico
Hispania noua
Mare Eoum
Cathaia
Ilandes of Molucca

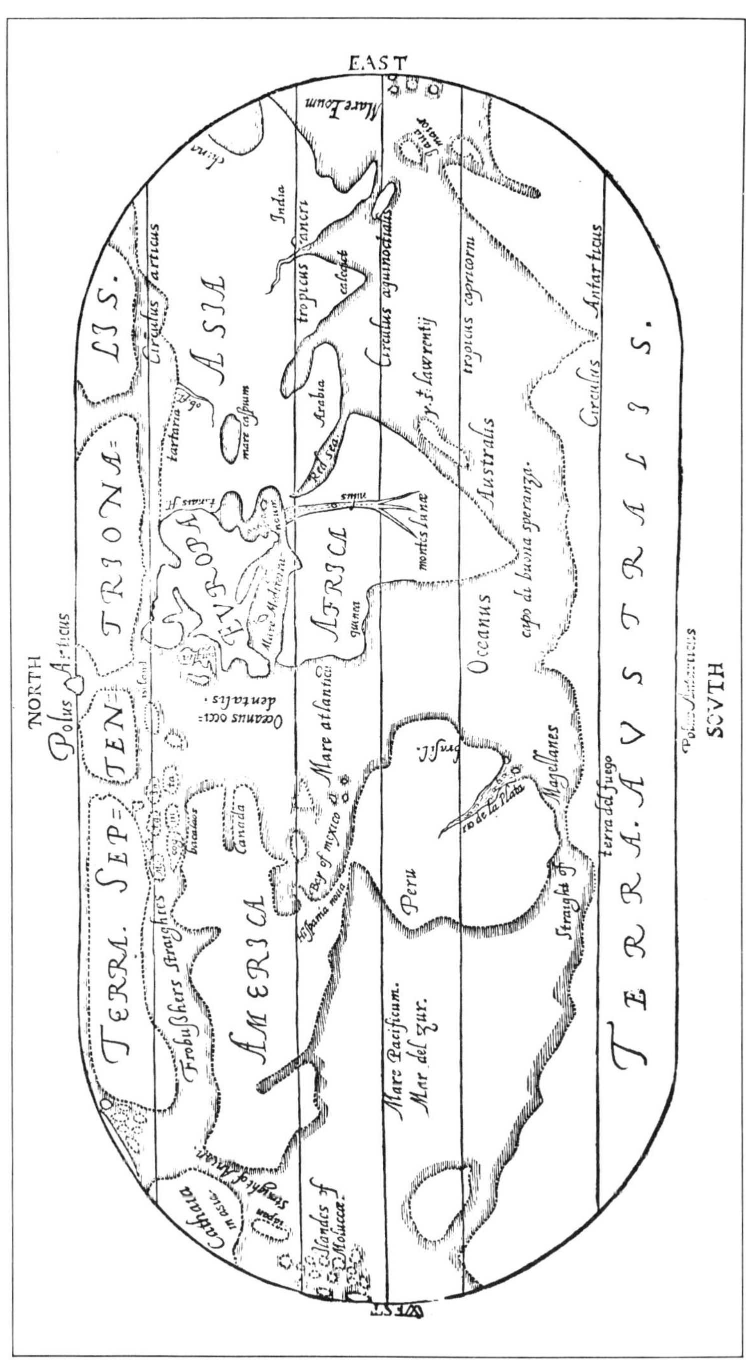

Figure 14

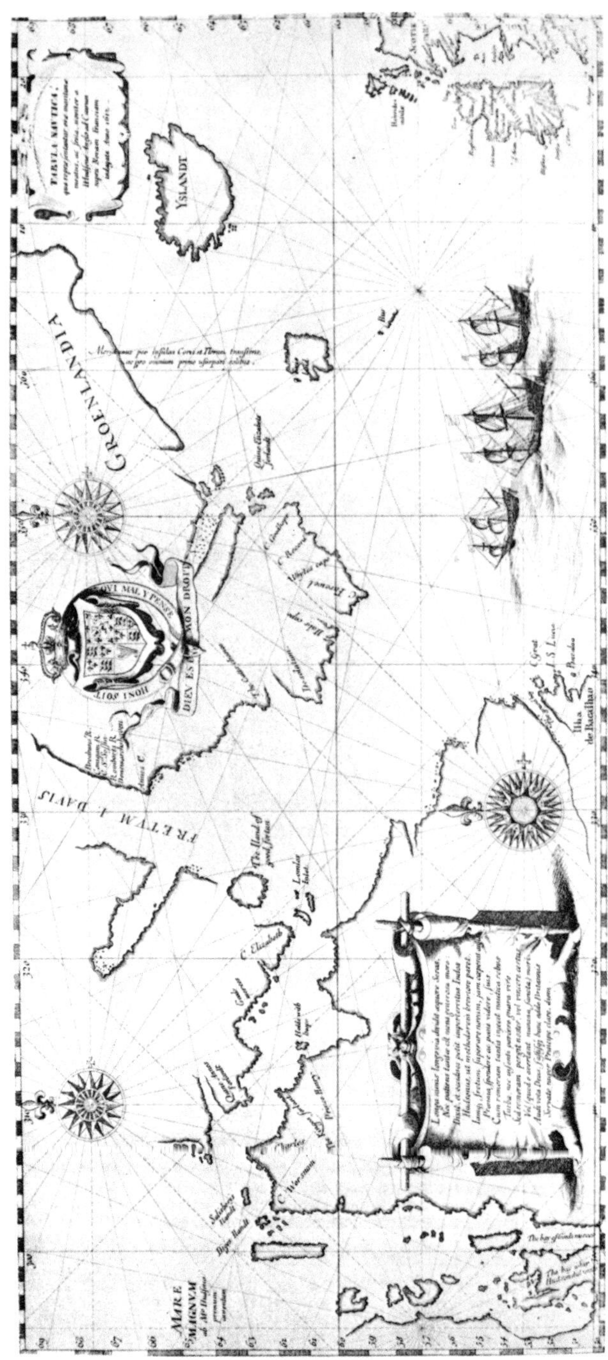


Figure 15

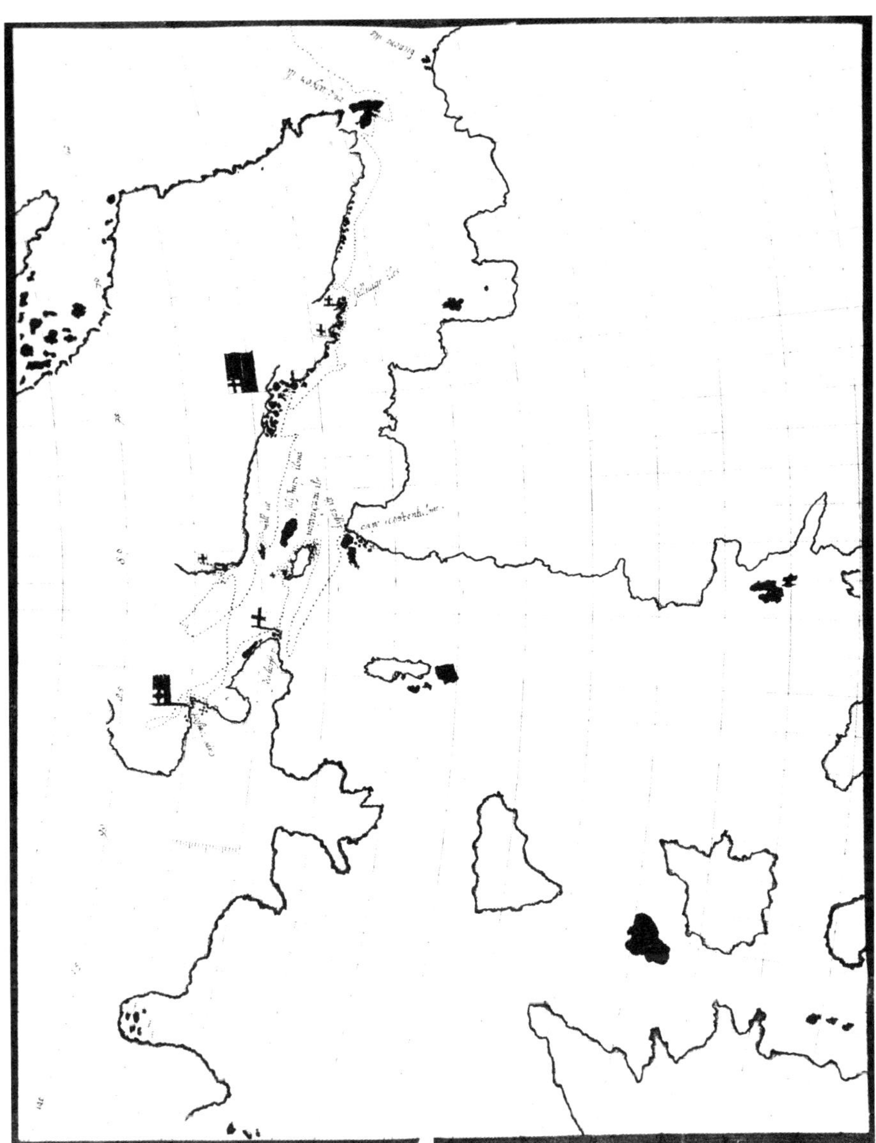

Figure 16

THE PLAN
or SAYLING
for the discovery
of a Passage into the
SOUTH SEA
1631. 1632.
Iceland
Scotland
England
Ireland
Freeland
C.Monmouth
C.Henrietta Maria
Baffins Bay
Terra La Brador
Buttons Bay
New North Wales
New South Wales

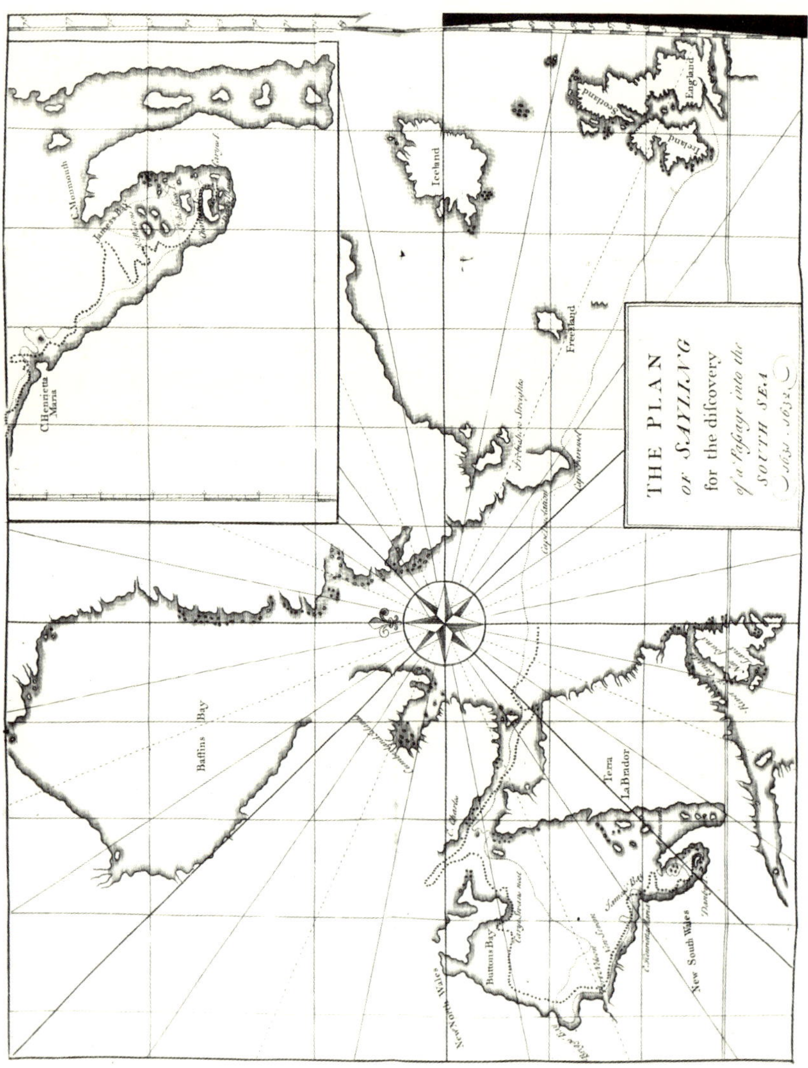

**Figure 17**

REGIONES
SVB POLO ARCTICO
Baffins Bay
Buttons Bay
NOVA BRITANNIA

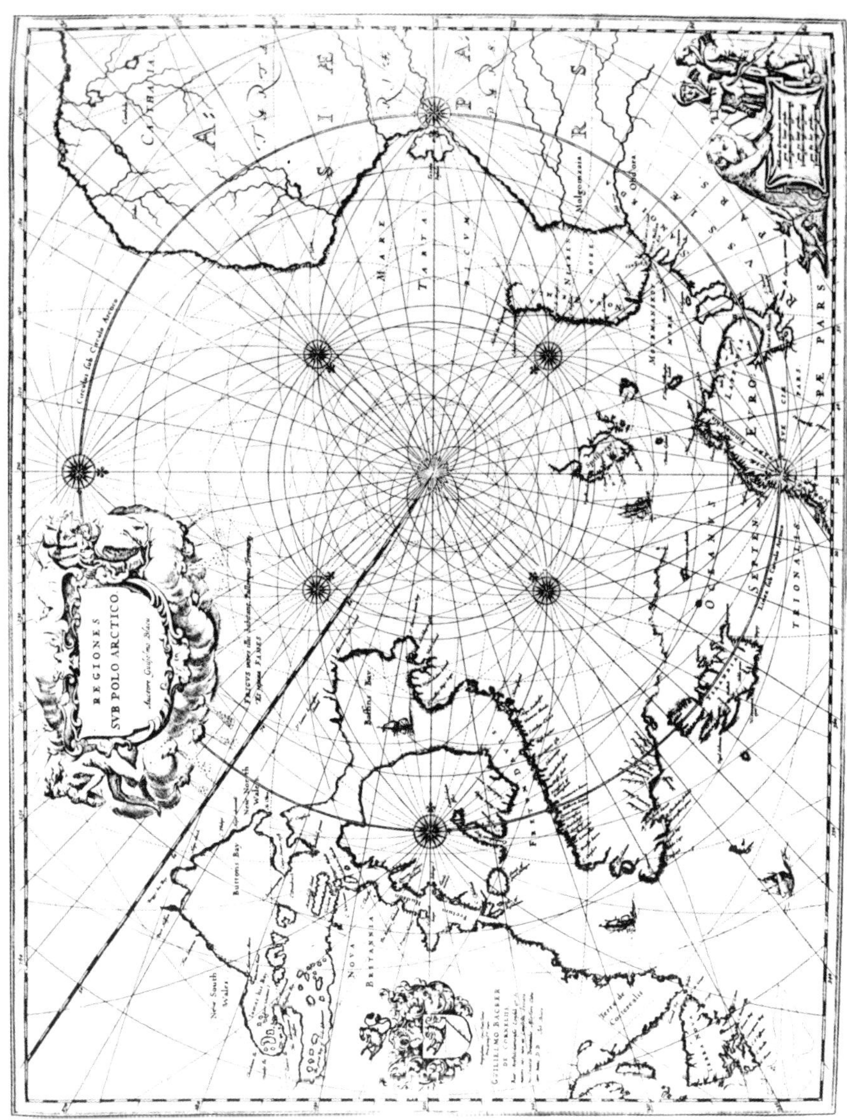

Figure 18

## Aftermath

DURING THE INITIAL SEARCH for a northwest passage, from 1576 to 1632, seventeen expeditions were fielded. We have examined these in some detail in the previous pages. To broaden our perspective, we will continue our narrative with a closer look at the ships that were used, and at the men who sailed them. We will also enquire into the methods that were used by the pilots to find their way across the trackless ocean.

### Vessels

ALTHOUGH no description of drawings of the vessels have survived, we still have a fairly good idea as to what they looked like. For example, we know that Weymouth's vessel, the *Discovery*, was a Dutch fly-boat or fluyt (Christy, 1894, p. 80). It differed from the English ships of the period in having a round tuck. English vessels of the same period had a square tuck or transom. We know, further, that the *Discovery* was a 70-ton vessel, which would suggest that it was 60-70 feet long. Its internal structure would approximate that of the English vessels we will discuss below. Apart from Weymouth's *Discovery* and Jens Munk's *Unicorn* and *Lamprey*, all of the vessels were small English merchantmen. There was no difference, incidentally, between a small merchant vessel and a small naval vessel at that time. In an emergency, when the national fleet had to be expanded in a hurry, the sovereign would simply charter or confiscate merchantmen, and increase their armament. For all sea-going vessels of the period were already armed with at least a few cannon. And in times of peace, the sovereign would frequently make the royal vessels available to private companies who would use them as merchantmen. As was noted earlier, one of Queen Elizabeth's vessels, the *Ayde*, was used by Martin Frobisher on his third voyage.

Our knowledge of sixteenth and seventeenth century vessels is derived largely from some documents that have fortunately survived. Foremost among these is a manuscript entitled *Fragments of Ancient English Shipwrightry*, possibly by Matthew Baker. It is in the Pepys Library,

Magdalene College, Cambridge, England. Others include a *Sea Grammar* by Captain John Smith, London, 1627; M. Oppenheimer's *Administration of the Royal Navy, 1509-1660,* London, 1890; and the anonymous leaflet called *A Treatise on Shipbuilding, 1620 1625.* These provide us with a wealth of details on the design and building of the hull, internal arrangements, and rigging of Elizabethan and Stewart ships. The length of these vessels, however, was almost never recorded. It seems odd to us that no one bothered to paint a picture of Drake's *Golden Hind,* for example, or took the trouble to record her dimensions. She was, after all, the first English vessel to encircle the globe. And in addition, she returned from her voyage heavily laden with treasure that Drake had taken from the Spaniards in the Pacific. Queen Elizabeth was so impressed with his achievements that she boarded the ship at Deptford, where she knighted Drake in 1581. At her command, the *Golden Hind* was preserved there, and put on public display. A dock was dug for the famous ship, and lined with brick-work. Although the dimensions of the vessel itself were never recorded, the bill for the brick-work has somehow survived. And the dimensions recorded there tell us the *Golden Hind* was no more than 66 feet long, and would have been rated at about 100 tons burden.

Information on three other vessels of the early seventeenth century is contained in an article on the *Design and Construction of the Jamestown Ships* These ships, the 100-ton *Susan Constant,* the 40-ton *Godspeed,* and the 20-ton pinnace, the *Discovery,* were owned by the Muscovy Company. They were charted by the Virginia Company in 1606 to found an English settlement in the New World. Sailing some 20 miles up the James River in what is now the state of Virginia, they anchored off a low but easily defended island. There, on 13 May 1607, they founded Jamestown, the first English colony in the United States.

In 1952 the Commonwealth of Virginia decided to build replicas of the three historic vessels, and have them ready for the 350th anniversary of the founding of Jamestown. To do the research and design the replicas, they selected G. C. Fee, a marine architect. Working from contemporary paintings of other seventeenth-century ships, and historical works on marine architecture, Fee was able to demonstrate that the length of the *Susan Constant* was about 80 feet, and corresponding measurements for the *Godspeed* and the *Discovery* were 50 and 39 feet. Although these figures do not tell us the size of the early ships that explored the Canadian Arctic, they do suggest an order of magnitude. Frobisher's *Ayde* then, would probably have been no longer than 70 or 80 feet, and all of the others would have been appreciably shorter. If we may hazard a generalization, it is very likely that most of the other vessels sailing into the northwest during the first phase of our arctic exploration were well under 50 feet in length.

Fortunately, we are on much firmer ground when we turn to the interior layout of the vessels and to their rigging. Apart from the smaller pinnaces, perhaps, they were all three-masted vessels and carried six sails. On both the mainmast and the foremast, they spread a mainsail or course, as well as a topsail; on the mizzenmast they spread a triangular lateen sail; and on a yard slung below the bowsprit, they carried a spritsail. This was the standard rig throughout most of the sixteenth and seventeenth century.

The interiors of the ships were also fairly standardized throughout the period. They had two decks running the length of the hull, the upper or main deck and the lower or orlop deck. Rising above the main deck were three superstructures, the forecastle in the bow, and the quarter deck and poop deck astern. Between the forecastle and the quarter deck bulkheads, or partitions, was the waist of the ship. Those who are unfamiliar with nautical terminology or marine architecture may find it less confusing to think of the small Elizabethan ship as a long, low two-story building with an extra story rising above the roof line at one end, the bow, and two extra stories at the other end, the stern.

The ground floor of the ship—to continue the comparison—was the hold which was covered by the orlop deck. A small, triangular compartment up the bow of the hold was the powder-room, where the gunner kept his gun-powder. There were also two other rooms in the bow as well, one for the bos'n's stores—such things as spare cables and anchors, rope, twine, paint and tar—the other for the carpenter's stores. At the stern were the bread-room and the steward's room. The mid-section of the hold was used for stowing cargo if the ship were on a trading mission, or for stowing additional supplies if she were engaged in exploration. There would have been some variation in these arrangements, of course, depending upon the nature of the voyage, the number of people aboard, the length of the voyage, the nature of the cargo, and similar variables.

The orlop deck on a small naval vessel was the fighting deck where the cannon were placed. Along each side was a row of square ports where the muzzles of the guns would be run out in a fight. Between battles, or when the vessel was engaged in trade, the ports would be closed with lids that were hinged at the top. The small merchantmen of the period, the ones that we are concerned with here, each mounted a few light cannon in the gun-r0w at the stern of the orlop deck. The centre of the deck, between the mainmast and the foremast, like that of the main deck above, was taken up with the large hatch through which cargo and supplies were lowered into the hold. In front of the hatch, that is towards the bow, was the capstan, a large windlass with a vertical drum that was used to winch in the anchor cables.

The main deck, like the orlop, ran the length of the vessel, from stern to gudgeon. Above the bow of this deck rose the forecastle, a superstructure that enclosed an area known as the chase. This area was usually used as a cook-room, or galley, as we would call it today. Farther aft, just abaft the mainmast, rose the quarter deck, reached by two sets of stairs, one on each side of the vessel, and separated from the waist of the ship by the quarter-deck bulkhead. Between the flights of stairs, a door led into the great cabin. This served as a dining-room, but it was also fitted with a few bunk beds, or standing cabins, as they were called at the time, and with lockers for storage. At the back of the great cabin stood the helmsman with his whip-staff. This was a vertical, wooden rod, pivoted at the deck so it could swing from side to side. Below the pivot, it extended into the gun-room, where it was fastened to the end of the tiller with an iron ring. The helmsman steered the ship by moving the staff from side to side. In front of the helmsman stood the 'bittacle,' which housed the compass. Behind the great cabin, and again above the gun-room, was the captain's cabin. And rising above the captain's cabin, at the stern of the quarter-deck was the round-house, or master's cabin. The deck above the round-house was the poop, reached by stairs rising from the quarter-deck.

A fleet of such ships was organized in the same way that a modern fleet is organized, except that a different terminology was employed. A modern fleet is led by an *admiral,* who sails in a *flagship.* In Elizabethan times, a fleet was led by a *general,* and the ship in which he sailed was called an *admiral.* The general's second-in-command was the *lieutenant-general,* who sailed in the *vice-admiral.* Ships of the period were commanded by *captains.* Unlike a modern captain, however, this officer was not necessarily a seaman. In Spanish and Portuguese ships of the period, for example, the captain was traditionally a nobleman, except, of course, in small traders and fishermen. In English ships, on the other hand, the captain usually *was* a seaman, even when he had a master aboard to see to the workings of the ship. That arrangement, incidentally, is the reason for having the master's cabin directly onto the quarter-deck, the operational centre of the vessel. In smaller ships, the functions of captain and master were often vested in a single individual who was referred to not as the captain but as the master (see Christy, 1894, p. 204 fn.).

## Personnel

SUPPLIES ON THESE VESSELS were checked as they came aboard by a *purser,* who was also responsible for their disbursement. That is, he kept a record of everything that came aboard, and where it had gone to if it were no longer aboard. This included all cargo and gear, as well as the food and beverages that were used up from day to day by the crew. Since even the smallest mer-

merchantman was armed with at least a cannon or two, a *gunner* was an essential member of every ship's company. A *cooper* was equally essential because most of the foodstuff was packed in barrels, as were such items as nails, gun-powder, water, oil and vinegar, as well as beer and wine. It was the cooper's job to see that the casks were sound, and to dismantle them as they became empty, for neater stowing. Another wood-worker aboard all vessels was the *carpenter*. Although he was called upon for all manner of joinery, his primary task was to look after the hull, to stop any leaks that might develop, and to repair any damage that the ship might suffer. During voyages of exploration he was also responsible for setting up the pinnaces that were usually carried in frame.

The *surgeon*—or chirurgion, as he was called at the time—had a single responsibility aboard ship, to look after the physical well-being of the ship's company. This included shaving and barbering the officers and men as required (Kenyon, 1975, p. 76), for at the time, surgeons were members of the *Company of Barber Surgeons*, incorporated 1461. Captain John Smith (1627, p. 34) tells us that:

> The Chirurgion is to be exempted from all duty but to attend the sick and cure the wounded; and good care would be had (that) he have a certificate from the Barber Chirurgion's Hall of his sufficiency, and also that his chest be well furnished both for Physicke and Chirurgery, and so neare as may be proper for that clime you goe for which neglect hath beene the losse of many a man's life.

On a larger ship, some or all of the above would have an assistant or *mate* as well. One of these men, the master's mate, or the first mate in modern parlance, was second in command of the vessel. These men, together with the bos'n, were the officers who ran the ship and looked after the interests of the owners. The cook on such a vessel was not an officer, but a member of the crew. He did his cooking in the forecastle or some other convenient place on a simple portable stove or hearth, usually no more than a shallow, iron box filled with sand. Only the largest vessels, like Frobisher's *Ayde*, had a brick-lined cook-room. In either event, the meals were simple and could be cooked only during good weather. During the storms that occurred so frequently in the Arctic the men ate their food cold.

Captain John Smith mentions another officer, the *marshall,* who does not appear on the crew-lists of early arctic explorers to my knowledge. In all probability, he would have served only on the larger naval vessels in time of war. His job was to see that offenders were properly punished for their infractions of the captain's regulations or naval orders. He is mentioned here only because the punishments he meted out were typical of the period. For example, an offender could be suspended by a rope reeved through a pulley at the end of one of the yards, and repeatedly dunked in the sea. A particularly nasty form of punishment was keel-hauling, in which the offender was trussed up at the end of a rope, then dragged under the ship from one side to the other. By all reports, this was not only uncomfortable, to say the least, it was also dangerous because the ship's hull would normally be covered with barnacles, which converted it into a very effective grater. Putting an offender in leg-irons was reserved for the most minor offences, as was beating the guilty party with a barrel-stave. Administered by an enthusiast, this form of punishment could produce an interesting pattern of welts on the offender, particularly if he was beaten with a stave that contained a bung-hole. In another common method of punishment, the miscreant was bound to the capstan or the main-mast with a basket of shot hung around his neck. And for very serious offences such as mutiny, an offender would be summarily hanged from a yard-arm.

## Diet

THE DIET OF ELIZABETHAN seamen was bread, beef and beer, the staple diet of England at the time. On shipboard, the bread was ship's biscuits, hard-tack, and was issued at the rate of one pound per man per day. Meat was issued at the same rate. And to wash it down, each man was issued one gallon of beer per day. In an England that had so recently been catholic, fish days were an accepted dietary practice.

We know that all the arctic expeditions we have examined in the preceding pages served meat on some days and fish on the others. But I have been unable to find any reference to the ratio of flesh days to fish days aboard Elizabethan ships. Richard Collinson, however, does provide us with an answer (1867, p. 105). In a confused but very interesting list of 'vittouls' that was drawn up in preparation for Frobisher's second voyage, in 1577, he tells us that 'Bieffe for 111 [sic] monthes having fleshe daies 48' was issued at the rate of '1 lb. a man per diem.' We know from the same document that their calculations were based on a month of 28 days. Three such months would then contain 84 days. Of these, we are told that 48 are 'fleshe daies; the remaining 36 would therefore be 'fishe daies.' The ratio of 48 to 36 is 4 to 3; each week would thus contain 4 flesh days and 3 fish days. The fish they served was dried cod, called 'stocke fishe,' and was issued at the rate of 1/4 fish per man per day. Food was issued to each 'mess'of four men, rather than to each individual. The men then divided it up among themselves. On flesh days a man's diet consisted of 1 pound of salt meat, either beef or pork, 1 pound of ship's biscuit, 1/2 pint of peas, and 1 gallon of beer. On half of the fish days, 1/4 pound of butter was added to the diet, and on the other half of the fish days, a half

In addition to the staples mentioned above, Frobisher's vessels also carried: 960 bushels of 'meale,' probably flour, which was packed in 240 barrels, each containing 4 bushels; 256 bushels of peas; 40 bushels of oatmeal; 125 pounds of rice; 1260 gallons of wine; 126 gallons of brandy; 252 gallons of honey; 63 gallons of 'sallet oyle,' probably olive oil; 252 gallons of vinegar; and 4 bushels of mustard-seed. We are told that the oatmeal was reserve stock, to be used in place of fish if the fish were to be used up before they got back to England. But much of the 'vittoules' must have been carried as reserve supplies. The vinegar, as well as the mustard-seed, was used as a relish on the salt meat. The vast quantity of vinegar that they carried is explained by the fact that it was also used as a disinfectant for cleaning the bilges. These had to be cleaned from time to time because the men would often use them instead of the toilet. This was against all regulations, of course, but the regulation was almost impossible to enforce. The toilet aboard a ship was either the beak-head or the chaines, both very uncomfortable places in wet weather, and dangerous as well. The men much preferred the bilges; they were protected, and were close at hand for a sailor who was off

Frobisher also had a small quantity of other food aboard, such things as 'proynes, 2 firkens [i.e., 15 gallons of prunes], reasons, almonds, liccores, etc.' These items were reserved for the sick, and were apparently prescribed by the surgeon.

Thomas James gives us some insight into how the food was prepared and served during the winter of 1631-32 on Charlton Island, in James Bay (Kenyon, 1975, p. 92). Although we do not have a list of the supplies he carried, we do know that his basic diet was the same as that of Frobisher's men some fifty years earlier. That is, James and his men lived almost entirely on beef, biscuit, fish, oatmeal and beer.

When we left England [he tells us] we were well-provided with beef, pork, fish, etc., which the cook now prepared in the following manner. The beef for Sunday night's supper he boiled on Saturday night in a kettle of water to which he had added a quart of oatmeal. After boiling the mixture for about an hour, he removed the beef and boiled down the broth until its volume was reduced by half. This we called porridge and ate with bread while it was as hot as we could stand. Following the porridge, we had our customary fish. For Sunday dinner we had pork and peas, and for supper the beef that had been formerly boiled, along with some more porridge. In like manner, the beef for Tuesday was boiled on Monday night, and Thursday's beef on Wednesday. Thus we had a warm supper in our bellies every night except Friday.

This rather confused menu leaves much to be desired, but it does tell us something. It tells us, for example, that they were eating two meals a day, rather than three. It tells us, further, that they boiled meat—either beef or pork—on Mondays, Wednesdays and Saturdays, and that they ate boiled meat the following day. But we also know from the Frobisher records that the food allowance was issued for the *day*, not the *meal*. That is, on a meat day, the men ate meat at every meal; and on fish days, they ate fish at every meal. James tells us that they ate hot porridge and bread, followed by fish, on Saturday. Therefore, Saturday was a fish day. It would appear, too, that Mondays and Wednesdays would be fish days as well, for on those days, too, the cook boiled meat for the following day. Monday, Wednesday, and Saturday, then, were fish days, while Tuesday, Thursday and Sundays were meat days. Because Friday was traditionally a fast day in predominantly catholic Europe, Friday was probably a fish day on Charlton Island as well.

## Ailments

WE WOULD EXPECT SEAMEN TO suffer severe bouts of scurvy if they kept to such a diet for any length of time, and this they surely did. We have detailed descriptions of that ailment among Jens Munk's crew that wintered at Churchill in 1619-20, and Thomas James' crew that wintered on Charlton Island in 1631-32. Button's men probably suffered from it as well, but all we know for sure is that he suffered a very high rate of mortality. All of the captains were acquainted with scurvy, as were all other seamen at that time. It was a well known and dreaded affliction. Everyone seemed to know that it would disappear if greens could be added to the diet; and most of them realized that fresh meat was an anti-scorbutic as well. But greens are hard to come by in the Arctic, and hunting would not have provided enough fresh meat for either James' crew or Munk's crew. For game was widely dispersed in the areas in which they wintered, and would have supported only a few people at any one spot. And in addition, the Europeans were not experienced hunters, nor did they have the necessary equipment to live off the land. Both parties, too, reported that their clothing was totally unsuited to the harsh continental climate to which they were exposed. As a result, both wintering parties were riddled with scurvy.

James described the illness as follows:

Soon after Christmas, many of the men were afflicted with such sore mouths that they could eat neither beef, pork, fish nor porridge. Their diet consisted mainly of bread or oatmeal which they pounded into flour in a mortar, then fried in a frying-pan with a little oil. Some would boil peas to a soft paste, and feed as well as they could on that. During the whole winter we took not more than a dozen foxes ... (which we) ... made into broth for the sick men who were weakest. Most of the men had sore mouths and loose teeth. Yet these sick and weary men had to work. So our surgeon—as diligent and sweet-tempered a man as I ever saw—would be at work early in the morning, picking the men's teeth, and cutting away the dead flesh from the gums (Kenyon, 1975, p. 93).

While the surgeon was working on their mouths, the men would bathe their swollen joints in a concoction that was brewed from 'trees, buds and herbs.' Had they but known it at the time, they could almost certainly have cured their scurvy if they had taken the concoction internally. But this, they did not know. So they continued the never-ending task of gathering fire-wood, having no choice in the matter; and at nightfall, the surgeon would have to repeat his ministrations 'before they sought the comfort of their beds. And thus did our miseries follow us all through the winter.' Apart from those who died of scurvy, however, only two men perished during the entire expedition, and both of those from accidents. James noted in his journal—with some wonder, apparently—'that none of us had been troubled that winter with any rheums or phlegmatic diseases.' That is, apart from scurvy, their health seems to have been excellent.

Eleven years before James' wintering on Charlton Island, Jens Munk had lost 62 men out of a party of 65 when he wintered at the mouth of the Churchill River. Much of that terrible mortality can be attributed to scurvy, but not all of it. Munk probably recognized the presence of scurvy and would certainly have been acquainted with its symptoms, but he never once used the word itself. However, he did describe the crew's symptom too clearly to permit of any doubt. Writing towards the end of May, 1620, Munk recorded the following observation:

There were only seven of us miserable people still alive, and we lay there day after day looking mournfully at each other, hoping that the snow would melt and that the ice would drift away. The illness that had fallen upon us was rare and extraordinary, with most peculiar symptoms. The limbs and joints were miserably drawn together, and there were great pains in the loins as of a thousand knives had been thrust there. At the same time, the body was discoloured as when someone has a black eye, and all the limbs were powerless. The mouth, too, was in a miserable condition, as all the teeth were loose, so that it was impossible to eat (Kenyon, 1980, p. 34).

These are the well known symptoms of scurvy, the same symptoms that were described by Thomas James. Not only was the ailment well known, but in all probability the cure—or one of the cures—was known as well. Thomas Woodall, surgeon-general to the East India Company, published a book called *The Surgeons Mate,* in which he tells us that 'scurvy is a disease of the spleen' (Woodall, 1617, p. 178). We are then told that:

Some judicious writers doe affirme this sicknesse to come by the melancholike humors gathered in *Vena Porta,* by which, it is sayd, the milt doth draw unto it melancholly humours, and so transporteth it from the milt into the ventricle. But truely the caused of this disease are so infinite and unsearchable as they farre passe my capacity to search them all out.

Woodall did understand, however, that scurvy was caused by a prolonged diet of salt meat. He understood, further, that it could be cured quite easily by adding fresh food to the diet. Commenting upon the appearance of scurvy during the long sea-voyages from England to the Cape of Good Hope, he tells us that 'at their comming on land there they presently grow strong againe & are by the very fresh ayre and fresh food cured without much other help.' Thomas James and Jens Munk must also have known that scurvy would respond to fresh food, for they both made every effort to secure fresh meat by hunting and trapping, and what little game they could take, they fed to the sick.

The other illness that afflicted Munk's party had symptoms that were completely different from those of scurvy. Munk's journal entry for 10 January 1620, reads as follows:

> On the tenth, Mr. Rasmus Jensen, the priest, and Mr. Casper Caspersen, the surgeon, took to their beds after having been ill for some time. That same day my head cook perished. And then a violent illness spread among the men, growing worse each day. It was a peculiar malady, in which the sick men were usually attacked by dysentery about three weeks before they died (Kenyon, 1980, p. 26).

This malady was probably trichinosis, an infection they caught from eating poorly cooked bear meat. The records are admittedly scanty, but we know they ate at least the one polar bear that they shot on 12 September. The bear was attracted by a small white whale, a beluga, that had been killed the previous day, and was still lying on the beach. Munk informs us that he 'gave the meat to the crew with orders that it was to be just slightly boiled, then kept in vinegar overnight.' Munk himself ate a piece of roasted bear meat, and pronounced it 'of good taste and quite agreeable.' But eating polar bear meat can be deadly—unless it is thoroughly cooked—for trichinosis is endemic to the Arctic.

It is significant, in all probability, that the expeditions that suffered unusually high mortality rated, those of Thomas Button and Jens Munk, both wintered in areas where polar bears were plentiful. Hudson and James, on the other hand, wintered in areas that were seldom visited by polar bears. Apart from what was probably trichinosis in two of the wintering parties, all of the early arctic explorers seem to have been remarkably healthy apart from scurvy. A few of Frobisher's men died from unknown causes, and were buried in the Arctic. The only disease mentioned by Frobisher was Morbus Gallicus, or syphilis, and this only as a passing remark (Kenyon, 1975, p. 117). We must not assume, however that because a disease was not mentioned, that it was not present. Frobisher, for example, does not mention scurvy on any of his arctic voyages, although it was certainly present, and probably widespread. He and the other officers no doubt accepted it as such a normal occurrence that no comment was required. Only

Edward Fenton, captain of the *Judith* on Frobisher's 1578 voyage, refers to scurvy specifically, and then only after his arrival back in England on 30 September. There, he tells us, he 'sett divers men on shoore and others willing to departe to their frindes, the Shippe being pestered with 67 men, the moste parte wherof infected with the skurvie and other daungerfull diseases' (Taylor, p. 64). When measuring the depredations of scurvy and other diseases throughout the crews of early arctic explorers, we must measure them against seventeenth century mortality rates, not twentieth century rates. When we do that, we find them much less singular, for we find that military authorities in the seventeenth century assumed that fifteen percent of their troops in barracks would die of natural causes in the course of a

## Clothing

SCURVY AND HARDSHIPS WERE simply an accepted part of the sailor's lot during the sixteenth and seventeenth centuries. The ice and snow encountered in arctic Canada, even during the summer, was an entirely different matter, however. English seamen had no experience in dealing with sub-zero temperatures, even those men who sailed to Lapland and the White Sea. And with no experience to guide them, they found themselves poorly equipped to deal with the climate of arctic Canada. In fact, James and Munk spent more time complaining of the cold than they did complaining of their ailments. There can be no doubt that their clothing was inadequate, for they were wearing the then current English costume of hose, breeches, shirt and doublet, with gowns and cassocks as outer garments. On their feet, they wore either boots or moccasin-like shoes. For headgear, they would sometimes wear high fur hats, but more commonly, the caps and berets of the period.

The East India Company, which dispatched George Weymouth into the northwest in 1602, kept meticulous records of its operations, and many such records have survived. They provide us with the only detailed information we have on the clothing of early arctic expedi-

for Weymouh is as follows (Rundall, 1849, pp. 59-60):

31 pair leather breeches lined with lambskin.
6 pair other breeches.
30 leather cassocks lined with lambskin.
30 leather hoods lined with lambskin.
30 leather gowns lines with frieze.
4 other gowns.
30 pair leather mittens lined with lambskin.
31 pair wadmal boot-hose.
32 pair frieze socks.
82 pair neat leather boots.
32 pair neat leather boots.
109 linen shirts.
47 cotton waistcoats.
12 pair 'knyt' woollen hose of sundry colours.
19 pair stockings.
48 dozen leather points.
7 pettycotes.
5 doublets.
6 mandillions.
3 white capoches.

We know from the same records that provide us with the list of clothing that the East India Company had the leather clothes specially made for the voyage. Such garments would normally have been made of coarse cloth for the lower classes of England, and of richer fabrics for the gentry. The use of leather was a concession—and the only concession—to the arctic climate. The garments themselves probably require a word or two of explanation. When donning his northern attire, the sailor would

**Figure 19** Woodcut illustration of a British sailor of the Elizabethan era, in garb suitable for Arctic voyages; note the fur cap, possibly made from a beaver pelt.

pull on a pair of long, cloth stockings, then a pair of the fleece-lined, leather breeches; these would cover the tops of the stockings, and were tied just below the knee. On his feet, he would wear either a pair of 'neat leather shoes' or a pair of 'neat leather boots.' The adjective 'neat' had nothing to do with neatness; it referred, rather, to leather that was made from the hides of domestic cattle. On his upper body, the seaman wore a long-sleeved shirt, probably collarless, over which he wore a waistcoat or petticoat. Although they are entered separately on the above list, these last two garments were essentially the same. They were close-fitting, quilted pieces of clothing that were worn under the doublet for warmth. The doublet itself, the usual jacket of the period, was a long-waisted upper garment with front closure and a short skirt flaring out over the hips. To keep the breeches from going adrift, they were laced to the hem of the doublet, under the skirt as a rule, with leather thongs known a 'points.'

The cassocks, gowns and mandilions were all overcoats. The cassock was a loose coat that widened towards the hem. It had front closure, and during Weymouth's time, reached only to the hips. The gown was a loose over-garment, open down the front, and reaching to the ankles; it survives today in academic gowns and judicial robes. The mandilion was a loose, thigh-length overcoat with a standing collar. It was buttoned down the chest only, and was slipped on over the head. A capoche was either a hood, such as is found on the habit of a monk, or a cape. In the present context, it was probably the latter.

## Wages

THE WAGES PAID TO THE OFFICERS and men on an arctic expedition of the period provide us with two different but related kinds of information. On the one hand, they provide us with a rough idea as to the standard of living at the time, provided, of course, that we have some information on current prices at the time. On the other hand, they also offer us some insight into the relative status of the different occupations during the Eliza-bethan and Stewart periods.

We find, for example, that on Weymouth's voyage of 1602, the preacher, at £3 per month, was making almost double the wages of the surgeon, at £1,13s per month. The captain of the *Godspeed*, William Cobreath, received £6 per month, and thus outranked both the preacher and the surgeon. The master—or captain, as we would call him today—received only £2,10s per month. The seamen were paid between £1,6s and £1,10s, with a median wage of £1,8s per month, or £16,16s per year (Rundall, 1849, pp. 238-39). Weymouth himself was not paid by the month. If he could prove at the end of the voyage 'that he hath passed through the Northwest passage into the East Indies, and arrived at any porte within the dominion of the kingdomes of Cataya, China, or Japan,' he was to receive 'the some of five hundred pounds of lawful English money without fraude or coven.' On the other hand, if he was unable to reach his destination he was to receive nothing.

Such sums of money are quite meaningless, of course, except in relation to their purchasing power at the time. Thus they become more meaningful when we learn that 100 dried Newfoundland cod could be purchased for 9s in 1581. In 1624, 44 lb. of standing rib roast of beef cost 5s.4d; 1 sheep, butchered, cost 13s; 1 lamb, also butchered, cost 6s; and 3 chickens could be had for only 2s. During the same period, 2 quarts. of claret and 3 pints of sherry were purchased for 2s.10d. In 1621, a canvas shirt cost 3s.4d; a wollen shirt was much more expensive, costing 15s; and Irish hose cost 2s.3d per pair. Ship's chandlers at the time were providing both beef and pork at 18s per cwt., flour at 13s per cwt., and ship's beer at 40s per tun (than is, at 40s per 252 gals.), or just over a penny per gallon (Rundall, 1849, pp. 244-45).

According to the standards of the day, early arctic explorers, both officers and men, were well paid and well fed. In addition to their board and lodging, they usually had a surgeon to attend to their physical ailments, and a preacher to watch over their spiritual welfare. They probably sailed to the Arctic for the same reason that young men go north today to build pipelines, and drill for gas and oil. They were drawn to the north by good wages and the chance of adventure. This was pointed out by Martin Frobisher at the conclusion of his second voyage in 1577. He said that he

> lost but a single person during the entire voyage, apart from one man who died at sea; and he was sick when he came aboard. But he was so anxious to join the expedition that he chose to die in the attempt rather than be excluded from so notable a voyage.

We should probably make some allowance for Elizabethan exuberance when evaluating such statements. After all, Frobisher was hardly an unbiased reporter. But his basic position was sound, for signing on crews for such a venture was never a problem.

## Navigation

OUTSIDE THE SIGHT OF LAND, the medieval pilots relied solely upon a knowledge of directions and distances to find their way from port to port. Their only navigational instrument was the compass. It had been used by European seamen since 1294 at least, for in that year, a compass appears on the inventory of the *San Nicola* (Taylor, 1971, p. 115). At that time, the pilots learned their trade through an apprenticeship system. Starting at the bottom as ship's boys or grommets, they slowly learned the ways of a ship. And experience taught them to recognize capes, headlands, estuaries and islands from any angle, and in a variety of light and weather conditions. As they worked their way up the ladder of authority, they in turn would train younger men in the mysteries of their craft. In this way, a knowledge of navigation was passed on from generation to generation, as it had been in Europe for countless centuries.

When the Portuguese started to push down the west coast of Africa in the mid-fifteenth century, however, they were following an uncharted coast along which both direction and distance were unknown. As a result, they had to devise some new method of fixing and recording their positions. By 1460, they had solved the problem; they adopted the quadrant that the astronomers used for measuring the declinations of celestial bodies. This was an awkward instrument for using at sea, however, so the pilot would go ashore from time to time, and fix his position by measuring the angular distance of the north star, *polaris,* above the horizontal plane. This figure he converted into degrees of latitude south from some place whose latitude was already known, usually Lisbon.

The quadrant itself was a quarter circle of wood or brass with a sighting vane at each end of one of the radii, and a plumb-bob suspended from the apex. The circular edge of the quadrant was graduated from 0 to 90 degrees. To determine his latitude, the pilot would sight *polaris* through the sighting vanes on his instrument while an assistant would read off the elevation. That is, he would read off the number on the graduated arc that was cut by the string on the plumb-bob.

As the Portuguese moved farther south, however, *polaris* dropped so close to the northern horizon that it could no longer be used as a navigational star. By 1481—the year they crossed the equator for the first time—the Portuguese were already using an astrolabe to determine their position by measuring the altitude of the sun. The astrolabe was a circular brass disc, again borrowed from the astronomers, graduated in degrees and minutes around its outer edge, and suspended by a brass ring at the top. A flat arm was pivoted in the centre of the instrument; and at each end of the arm was a small raised lug with a pin-hole in its centre. The pilot could determine the elevation of a celestial body by sighting it through the pin-holes, and reading its elevation from the graduated scale. When using the astrolabe to measure the elevation of the sun, he usually found it more convenient to line up the vane so that a ray of sunlight would shine through the two pin-holed, and land on his hand or some conveniently held object. Like the quadrant, which continued in use for some time, the astrolabe was an awkward instrument unless it, too, were taken ashore, where it could be held steady. The earliest reference to the use of an astrolabe at sea is 1481.

The pilots of the fifteenth century had borrowed both the quadrant and the astrolabe from the astronomers, as we have seen. The next instrument that was used for measuring celestial angles was the cross-staff, the first such instrument that was developed by the seamen themselves. It consisted of a slender, graduated staff, to which was affixed a sliding cross-member. To measure the altitude of a celestial body—usually the sun—one end of the staff was held beside the eye, while the sliding member was moved until one end rested on the horizon, and the other end rested on the sun. The angle between them was then read from the graduated staff. Although the cross-staff was much easier to use aboard ship than either the quadrant or the astrolabe, it did present serious problems. First, it forced the pilot to look directly at the sun, and second, it required the pilot to look in two different directions at the same time—at the horizon and at the sun. In spite of such drawbacks, however, the cross-staff, and its derivative, the back-staff, continued in use from its first appearance in the early 1500s until John Hadley's *octant* was tested and approved by the Lords Commissioners of the Navy in 1732 (Taylor, 1971, p. 257).

While Spain and Portugal were sailing unknown seas, and establishing their overseas empires, England was left in a technological backwater. Her seamen were still restricted to the Mediterranean and the west coast of Europe. The English merchants finally realized that the key to success in an era of expanding horizons and markers was celestial navigation. And for this they needed seamen who had been trained in basic astronomy, in the use of astronomical tables, and in the use of the navigational instruments—the quadrant, astrolabe, and above all, the cross-staff. And these were not skills that an illiterate seaman could pick up during his apprenticeship at sea. Such skills could be acquired only through formal instruction. To train Englishmen in the mysteries of the new navigation, a group of influential merchants persuaded Sebastian Cabot to give up his post as Chief Pilot of Spain, and return to London in 1548.

In mapping the heavens, the astronomers of the period were using a system of celestial co-ordinates that is symmetrical with the system of geographic co-ordinates that we use today. That is, they saw the heavens as a celestial sphere with the earth at its centre. Projected into infinite space, the poles of the earth, both north and south, became the poles of the celestial sphere. The equator, too, was projected outward to form a celestial equator. They knew, of course, that the earth was not at the centre of the solar system. But such a model provided them with the fixed coordinates that the heavenly mapping required. Using this system, the astronomical latitude of a heavenly body such as the sun was its angular distance north or south of the equator. Astronomers and navigators, incidentally, refer to the latitude of a celestial body as its *declination.* But the sun's declination changes constantly throughout the year. At the spring equinox, about 21 March, it is directly over the equator. From there, it moves steadily northward until it reaches through the Tropic of Cancer at 23.5° north. It arrives there about 21 June, at which time we in the northern hemisphere see it riding high in the summer sky. It is this northward movement of the sun, of course, that brings summer to those in the northern hemisphere at the same time that it brings winter to those in the southern hemisphere.

Sebastian Cabot taught the sixteenth century navigators to think in terms of latitude and longitude, and to use the declination tables that the astronomers had drawn up to determine his latitude. The process was as follows. To find his latitude, the northern explorer would first measure the angular distance between the sun and the horizon at noon, when the angle was greatest. He did not require an accurate time-piece—or any time-piece, for that matter—because noon occurs at any point in the northern hemisphere when the angle between the sun and the southern horizon is greatest. Next, he subtracted the measured angle from 90°. The resulting figure was his zenith distance, that is, the angular distance between the sun and his zenith, the point on the celestial sphere that was directly above him. He then consulted his nautical almanac to find the sun's declination on that day. All he had to do then was to add his zenith distance to the declination of the sun. The result was his latitude. If, for example, the pilot of a vessel in the North Atlantic found that the sun, at noon, was 66°38' above the horizon, his zenith distance would be 90 minus 66°38', or 23°22'. Consulting his nautical almanac, he would then note the sun's declination for that day—say 21°17'. Adding his zenith distance and the sun's declination (23°22' + 21°17') gave him his position, 44°39' north.

But that position is not a specific point on the map. It is a parallel of latitude, an imaginary line that encircles the earth parallel to the equator. This particular parallel, by the way, stretches across the north Atlantic from Halifax, in Canada, to the Ferret Lighthouse on the coast of France, 12 miles south of Bordeaux. The early navigators used this ability to determine his latitude to practice what he called parallel sailing. Wanting to go to a particular port, he would sail either north or south, whichever was required, until he reached the latitude of that port, then follow a compass course east or west as the case may be, until he reached his destination. An experienced pilot who could estimate the speed and drift of his vessel would have some idea as to the position of his vessel at any given time. He would have no more than a very rough idea, however, because he had no way of determining his longitude, that is, his angular distance east or west of some known spot. He would have kept a record—a log—of the time spent on each compass corse, and this, with an estimate of the vessel's speed on each course, would give him what is known as a dead reckoning position. But a few days on the turbulent north Atlantic, particularly under overcast skies, would introduce a very large element of doubt into any such reckoning.

There was, however, a crude method of measuring the speed of a vessel, a method that had probably been in use for centuries. It entailed nothing more complicated than tossing a small piece of wood off the bow of a vessel, and measuring the time it took to appear off the stern. If a piece of wood were tossed off the bow of a fifty-foot vessel, for example, and was off the stern six seconds late, the vessel was obviously moving at the rate of fifty feet in six seconds or five hundred feet per minute, or thirty thousand feet per hour. As there are about six thousand feet in a nautical mile, the speed of

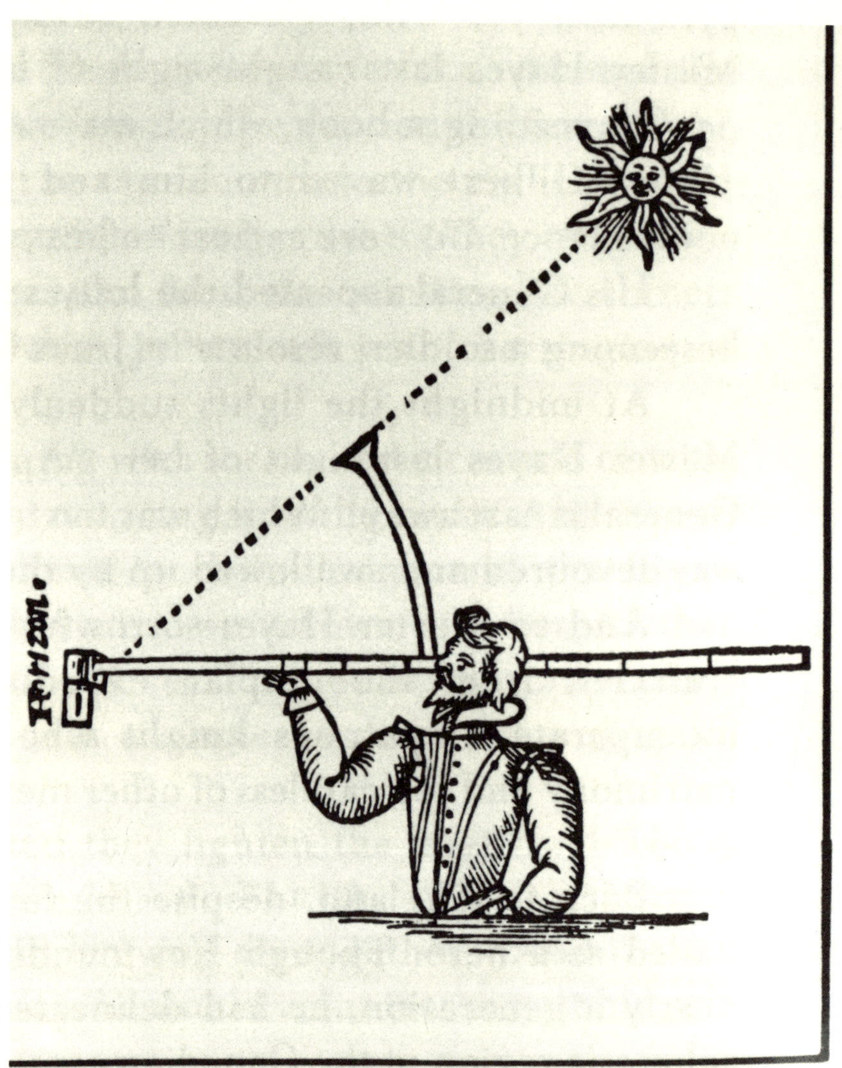

**Figure 20** The Davis backstaff quadrant, invented by the Arctic explorer John Davis (c. 1552-1605). From a woodcut in Davis's *Seaman's Secrets* (London, 1594), edited by A. H. Markham (London: The Hakluyt Society, 1878). Courtesy, The Hakluyt Society, London.

the vessel was five nautical miles per hour, or five knots. A refinement on this method was to fasten a line to the piece of wood, and stream it off the stern. For this, they used a small, triangular piece of wood with a thin strip of lead along the bottom to keep it upright in the water. Three short lines, one to each corner of the triangle, were tied together to form a yoke. The yoke was then tied to the end of a long line that was knotted at regular intervals. The speed of the vessel was then determined by streaming the triangular piece of wood, called the *chip*, from the stern of the vessel, and counting the number of knots that passed over the stern in a given length of time. This whole apparatus, by the way, was called a log-line. If we were to stream the log from the fifty-foot vessel used in the previous example, and use a line that was knotted at ten foot intervals, five of the knots would pass over the stern of the vessel in six seconds because she was travelling at five knots. This process can be summarized as follows: to calculate the speed of his ship, the pilot would count the number of knots in his log-line that passed over the stern in a given length of time, then multiply that number by the distance between the knots, measured in feet. The use of the term *knot* to describe a nautical rate of speed was derived from this practice. Although the log-line was used for a long time to measure the speed of vessels, many pilots felt that their own estimate, based on years of experience, was more reliable. Captain John Smith (1627, p. 55), for example, tells us that 'some use the log line, and a minute glass to know what way she makes, but that is so uncertain it is not worth the trouble to trie it.' Smith was probably right.

## Shipboard Routine

LIFE ABOARD A SIXTEENTH OR seventeenth-century vessel was dominated by a shipboard routine that was already ancient when Frobisher first sailed into th northwest. The nautical day started at 12 o'clock, noon, rather than at midnight as it did on land, because noon could be determined at sea, at least on a clear day, while midnight could not. It is noon for an observer in the northern hemisphere when the sun reaches its maximum elevation above the southern horizon. This, as we have seen, was measured with a cross-staff. When the sun reached its highest elevation, it was on the same meridian as the observer, and its bearing was due south. The nautical day, therefore, was from noon to noon. Carefully graduated sand-glasses then divided the day into hours and half hours. On a larger vessel, it was the duty of the ship's boys, or grommets, to turn the glasses at the instant the sand ran out. On smaller vessels, the helmsman would usually turn the small, half-hour glass. At each turn, he would give the ship's bell the appropriate number of strokes, starting with one bell at the end of the first half hour of the watch period. Adding one additional stroke at the end of each half hour, he would strike 'eight bells' at the end of the four-hour watch, then start over with 'one bell' to mark the end of the first half hour on the next watch. Each time he struck the bell, the helmsman would also lace another peg in the appropriate rhumb-line on his travers-board to record another half hour sailed of that course. These data were entered into the ship's log from time to time, and were used by the pilot to mark the position of the vessel on the chart. And this as we saw, was calculated for each day at noon, weather permitting.

At the start of a voyage, as soon as the full crew was aboard, the men were divided into two groups, the *starboard* watch, led by the master, and the *larboard* watch, or *port* watch as it is called today, led by the first mate. Captain John Smith (Goell, 1970, p. 48) explains that with the crew assembled on deck, the master would choose a man for his watch; the mate would then choose a man for his watch. They continued making alternate choices until the whole crew had been divided into two equal groups. This, incidentally, explains why ships usually carried an even number of crew-numbers. The watches then worked alternate shifts, four hours on and four hours off (Goell, 1970, p. 49). When the vessel was at anchor in a safe port, the men stood what they called 'quarter watch,' with only one quarter of the shift actually on duty at any one time. This gave the men some additional hours of leisure, and helped to compensate for the number of times that all hands were turned out for extra duty during a storm or other emergency. Once the watches were established, the men quickly settled into the nautical routine.

As soon as the watches were chosen, they were each divided into *messes* of four, five or six men, usually four. (This is the origin of the officer's mess, the sergeant's mess and the enlisted men's mess in the armed forced today.) Then, Smith tells us, the master should issue to each mess 'a quarter can of beere and a basket of bread to stay their stomacks until the kettle be boiled, that they may first goe to prayer, then to supper.' After a song and a prayer, the first watch then went on duty. Throughout the voyage, the watches would alternate, with each new watch marking its appearance with a song and a prayer.

Since time immemorial, sailors have been a superstitious lot, and deeply religious as well. Ship-owners of the Elizabethan and early Stewart times, who were equally devout, usually insisted that religious observances be strictly adhered to. Sebastian Cabot, for example, drew up a list of ordinances that were to be followed by the crews of the three ships that the newly formed Muscovy Company was sending to search for a northeast passage in 1553. Most of the regulations, of course, dealt with the company's business, systems of navigations, and similar matters. Ordinance number 12, however, is vividly explicit in its condemnation of most of the sins that a ship's crew might hope to be tempted with upon the high seas (Hakluyt, 1927, Vol. 1:225). It orders that:

> no blaspheming of God, or detestable swearing be used in any ship, nor communication of ribaldrie, filthy tales, or ungodly talke to be suffred in the company of any ship, neither dicing, carding, tabling, nor other develish games to be frequented, whereby ensueth not onely povertie to the players, but also strife, variance, brauling, and oftentimes murther to the utter destruction of the parties, and provoking of God's most just wrath, and sworde of vengeance. These and all such like pestilences, and contagions of vices, and sinnes to bee eschewed, and the offenders once monished, and not reforming, to bee punished at the discretion of the captaine and master, as appertaineth.

Having admonished the men to give up their evil practices, Cabot moves on, in his next ordinance, to an equally vigorous pursuit of God's benevolence. He decrees:

> that morning and evening prayer, with other common services appointed by the kings Majestie, and lawes of this Realme to be read and said in every ship by the minister in the Admirall (i.e., the flagship), and the merchant or some other person learned in other ships, and the Bible or paraphrases to be read devoutly and Christianly to Gods honour, and for his grace to be obtained, and had by humble and heartie praier of the Navigants accordingly.

The entire shipboard routine was thus dominated by two paramount considerations, the dread benevolence of God and the regularity that was introduced into human affairs by the sand glass. The first of these, the dependence of man upon the whims of a supreme being, was common to all of Christian Europe. But the regularities introduced by the sand glass shaped the affairs of seamen into a new rhythm, one that had not previously been felt. The lives of most earlier peoples had been regulated largely by natural mechanisms. Man's daily rhythms, for example, had been controlled for millennia by the sun's rising and setting, as was still true of men in other walks of life. Longer temporal cycles had been marked by the passing seasons. But now, for the first time, the lives of a large group of men were shaped into uniform periods of work and rest—four hours on, and four hours off—and these periods were measured by an inexorable trickle of sand. Today, we slice up the flow of time into homogenized units, and measure them with digital precision. The sand glass that first introduced these units into the affairs of men is vaguely remembered, however. When we say that 'time is running out' we are harking back to an earlier period, and noting that there is very little sand left in the glass.

### Other Explorers & Argonauts

AS WAS MENTIONED EARLIER, there was a gap of 185 years between the end of Phase I and the beginning of Pahse II in the exploration of the Canadian Arctic. Phase I, as we saw, ended when

Thomas James returned to England in 1632, after wintering on Charlton Island. Phase II was inaugurated in 1818 with the voyage of John Ross and W. E. Parry. Although there was no systematic search for a northwest passage between those dates, several important discoveries were made during that period, discoveries that are directly germane to the present discussion. The first of these was the voyage of a Siberian cossack named Semen Dezhnev (1981). In 1648 Dezhnev and a group of explorers, traders and hunters sailed east from the mouth of the Kolyma River in Siberia. Following the coast, they finally rounded a rocky promontory and continued south to the mouth of the Anadyr River. Dezhnev's voyage was of immense geographical importance because it demonstrated for the first time that Asia and America were two separate continents. Unfortunately, however, Dezhnev was illiterate, and totally unaware of the significance of his feat. A few brief notes, dictated by Dezhnev, were found in the regional archives in Yakutsk in 1736, but almost nothing else has

When Vitus Bering sailed north from the Kamchatka Peninsula in July, 1728, he was apparently expecting to find an isthmus connecting Asia and America, for the prevailing opinion at the time held that such an isthmus probably existed (Dezhnev, 198, p2). Having sailed through the strait that now bears his name, however, he found that the coast he was following was *not* joined to the Americas, nor did it continue north; it angled off to the northwest, just as the native Siberians, remembering the remarkable voyage of Semen Dezhnev, had told him it would.

In 1776, the British admiralty sent an expedition to the north Pacific to see if the northwest passage could by navigated from that direction. The expedition, consisting of two vessels, was led by Captain James Cook in the *Resolution*; the other vessel, under Captain Charles Clarke, was the *Discovery*. Two years later, on 9 August 1778, he reached Cape Prince of Wales on the eastern side of Bering Strait. Crossing to East Cape, the Siberian side of the strait, he headed northeast for Davis Strait, some 2500 miles to the east, but it was not to be. He soon reached the edge of the arctic pack, a barrier that 'rose like a solid wall ten or twelve feet above the water' (Beaglehole, 1974, p. 618). Following the edge of the pack to the east, he was forced to retreat in mid-August when the ice closed in on a point he named Icy Cape. Sailing westward from there, he followed the Siberian coast to North Cape, where his passage was again blocked by the pack. He had no choice then but to turn south into the Pacific. He wintered in Hawaii, where he was killed in a scuffle with the natives on 14 February 1779.

At Cook's death, Captain Charles Clarke assumed command of the expedition, and appointed first lieutenant John Gore as captain of the *Resolution*. After prolonged discussion, it was agreed that the expedition should attempt once again to return home by way of the Arctic Ocean, but again they were stopped by the solid arctic pack. On their passage through Bering Strait on 5 July, Clarke and his men were treated to a sight that had been denied to Dezhnev, Bering and even Cook himself:

> The weather becoming clear, we had the opportunity of seeing, at the same moment, the remarkable peaked hill near Cape Prince of Wales, on the coast of America, and the East Cape of Asia, with the two connecting islands of Saint Diomede between them (Cook, 1784, p. 244).

Far to the east, meanwhile, the Hudson's Bay Company had been caught up in northern exploration. It all began when James Knight, the Governor at York Factory, sailed north to the mouth of the Churchill River in 1717 to build a fort and establish trade relationships with the natives of the area. When some of the northern Indians arrived at Fort Prince of Wales, as it was called, they had lumps of native copper with them, as well as tools, weapons and ornaments fashioned from the same material. Knight enquired as to its origin, and learned that the Indians picked it up far to the northwest, near a large body of water that could have been either the western sea or the Arctic Ocean. In either event, the report was of interest, for the natives had enough copper to suggest that the ore body night be sufficiently large to support commercial development. Collecting a number of copper items from the Indians,

Knight sailed for England the following year. He showed his assortment of copper to the company directors, and suggested that they send him up to the northwest corner of Hudson Bay in order to find a passage through to the mines. When he got there, he would lade his vessels with copper and such other minerals as might be found in the area. He did not have any samples of gold with him, but the directors were apparently convinced that he would find some, for they not only accepted Knight's proposal, but supplied him with a number of iron-bound oak chests in which to store such treasure.

In spite of the fact that Knight was in his late seventies at the time, neither he nor the company directors had any doubts as to his ability to carry out the project. Knight, after all, spent most of his adult life with the company; having joining them as a shipwright and carpenter in 1676, he had worked his way steadily upward over the years. After serving as governor of several different posts on Hudson Bay and James Bay, he was finally appointed to the board of directors of the company, or the Committee, as it was usually called. Knight, at the time, was the only member of the committee with actual experience in the bay; he was a well-respected elder statesman, and successfully overcame any objections that the Governor or other committee members might have entertained. He was finally equipped with two sturdy vessels, the *Albany* and the *Discovery*, was well provisioned, and was instructed as follows: first, he was to search out the eastern entrance to the northwest passage—or the Straits of Anian, as it was called at the time. This, he was told, would probably be found on the west side of Roe's Welcome north of 64° north. He was then to sail westward in order to 'increase the company's trade, to locate gold and copper mines, and to establish a whaling industry' (DCB, Vol. 2:320). Knight and his party sailed from Gravesend on 4 June 1719, and were never seen again.

When he failed to return in 1720, it was thought that he may have located the passage, and sailed through to the Pacific. Or perhaps he had wintered his richly laden vessels in some convenient cove far to the northwest, and would appear in his own good time. By the spring of 1721, however, the company was sufficiently concerned to send out a search party. It sent Captain John Scroggs in the *Whalebone*, with orders to winter at Churchill, and sail north the following spring. The company made a poor choice when they chose Scroggs to carry out the search, for he was a rather inept navigator and an indifferent explorer. When he sailed up the coast from Churchill in 1722, he was accompanied by Richard Norton, an old company hand who acted as interpreter. Scroggs sailed north as far as Whalebone Point, near the upper end of Roe's Welcome, and then returned to Churchill. On his way south, he sailed past the entrance to Chesterfield Inlet, a broad, enticing channel leading due west, but ignored it completely, even after Norton had pointed it out to him. In spite of the cursory manner in which Scroggs examined the coast, he did manage to learn the fate of the Knight expedition. Near the eastern end of Marble Island he found a harbour in which the wrecks of the *Albany* and the *Discovery* were clearly visible, as were the scattered remains of the expedition party on shore. Scroggs reported 'that Every Man was killed by the Eskemoes.' Over the following years, men sailed north from Churchill almost every summer to trade with the natives at Whale Cove, the modern Term Point. From such men and from various Eskimo reports, and particularly form Samuel Hearne's visit of 1769, the following story was pieced together.

Knight and his party arrived at Marble Island in the late fall of 1719, having no doubt spent the previous weeks in unsuccessful exploration to the north. He probably chose Marble Island as a wintering-place because it provided a safe anchorage, and because it was some sixteen miles off the coast. This last feature would have been particularly important because the relationships between the company men and the Eskimo along the coast were still unsettled. The ships were safely moored in the small harbour. Food, coal and building materials were unloaded from the vessels, and a house measuring 29' x 47' was erected. The Eskimo reported that there were about fifty men on the island in the fall of 1719. 'By spring, their number were greatly reduced and by the end of the second winter only twenty men survived. Five lived until the summer of 1721 when they, too, died' (DCB, Vol.2:320). The last two to perish were the carpenter and the blacksmith.

This tragic series of events has never been satisfactorily explained. Although many members of the expedition were probably suffering from scurvy by the time they arrived at their wintering-place, they still had enough strength to build what appears to have been a large, substantial house; and we know from Hearne's report that many of the men, and perhaps the majority of them, lived through the first winter. Why, then, did they not sail down the coast to Churchill during the summer of 1720 or even 1721? Several members of the expedition were acquainted with the coast to the south, and they knew that it was no more than two hundred miles or so the Churchill. It is possible, of course, that they were attacked by the Eskimo during the summer of 1720, for Scroggs mentions such an attack, although he does not tell us when it occurred. In any event, the party was not wiped out, for we are told that twenty men were still alive at the end of the second winter. Although the ships themselves may have been damaged by the ice when they were frozen in, the survivors had the necessary tools, materials and skills to build a launch that would have carried them to safety. They can hardly have suffered greater depredations than were visited upon Jens Munk on that same coast one hundred years earlier. Yet Munk and two of his men managed to fight their way back to Norway. At least some of Knights men should have been able to manage the relatively short trip down the coast to Churchill. But they didn't move—or perhaps they couldn't. Through two long winters they tended the sick and the dying; and through two brief arctic summers, the survivors must have gazed out to sea, watching for a sail to appear on the horizon. But nothing appeared.

Continued trading voyages to the north of Churchill during the next few years failed to add anything significant to our knowledge of the area. Then in 1741, the British government, re-

responding to the political pressure of one Arthur Dobbs, sent Captain Christopher Middleton in *HMS Furnace* and Captain William Moor in *HMS Discovery* to search for a passage through Roes Welcome. Dobbs was a wealthy Irishman, High Sheriff of Antrim Country, Engineer-in-Chief and Surveyor General of Ireland. He was also the mayor of Carrickfergus where his ancestral home, Dobbs Castle, was located. Dobbs was convinced that the northwest passage could be found by sailing north through Roes Welcome, and that the Hudson's Bay Company had refused to explore that area more thoroughly in order to protect its monopoly. For once the passage were found, it would attract other merchants to the region, and this would surely break the monopoly that the company enjoyed. Dobbs, of course, wanted the area thrown open to all British merchants. That is, he wanted a piece of the action. And he had enough political clout to get the attention of powerful people in London.

Having gained the support of the government, Dobbs was certain that the company monopoly would soon be broken. For one, the *Furnace* and the *Discovery* had breached the barrier of ice that guarded the northwest passage, company control of the area would have been breached as well. He considered himself fortunate, too, in his choice of captains to lead the expedition. Both Middleton and Moor were personal friends of his; they were also old Company servants—as employees of the company were called at the time—and knew the country well. It was with high hopes, then, that the Middleton expedition sailed from London on 8 June 1741. After a scurvy-infested wintering at Churchill, the party headed north up the coast. On 12 July 1742, Middleton passed Whalebone point at 65° north, and entered unexplored territory for the first time. Later that same day he reached a cape that they prudently name Cape Dobbs. They were stopped at the cape by the ice, but were able to send the ship's boats ahead to explore a broad passage opening to the west. After a thorough examination that lasted two weeks, Middleton realized that the opening was not a strait, as they had hoped, but only a deep inlet. He named the inlet Wager Bay after Sir Charles Wager, First

Lord of the Admiralty. On 4 August, they again moved north until they discovered Repulse Bay, nestling just under the arctic circle. But the entire area was blocked with ice that swept into the bay from the east, from an ice-choked passage that he named Frozen Strait. Since there was no hope of a westward passage through Repulse Bay, and since the route to the north was solidly blocked by the ice, Middleton sailed for home.

Infuriated by Middleton's lack of success, Dobbs launched a vitriolic attack on that competent and honest seaman. The government finally realized that Dobbs was being vindictive and unreasonable, and therefore refused to lend further support to his schemes. Dobbs had enough support for his views, however, that he was able to raise £10,000 by public subscription. But it was such a slow, uphill effort that his next expedition did not sail until 1746. William Moor, Middleton's consort on the earlier voyage, was chosen to lead the party in the 180-ton *Dobbs;* a second vessel, the 140-ton *California,* was commanded by Francis Smith. Smith was an old company servant who had sailed a trading sloop from Churchill north to Whale Cove every summer from 1738 to 1744, except 1741 (Cooke and Holland, 1978, pp. 60-64). Both of these men, then, were old arctic hands who were thoroughly at home on the west side of Hudson Bay. Dobbs instructed them to make a detailed examination of Wager Bay—which he persistently called Wager Strait—because he believed that inlet to be the entrance to the northwest passage. The ships sailed from London on 10 May 1746. During the night of 21 June, the *Dobbs* was almost destroyed by a fire that broke out in the great cabin. It was finally brought under control by a bucket-brigade, but it very nearly broke through to the powder-room, which was directly below, and which was filled with thirty or forty barrels of gunpowder, as well as alcohol, candles, matches and other highly inflammable materials.

Apart from the fire, it was an uneventful crossing. They raised the coast of Resolution Island on 8 July while they were dodging icebergs that they described as 'Mountains of Ice.' Inside Hudson Strait, they encountered the usual assortment of pack-ice, fog and contrary winds. Both Moor and Smith were accustomed to dealing with such problems, however, and pushed slowly but steadily westward. On 26 August, they were anchored in Five Fathom Hole, at the mouth of the Hays River, and some seven miles below York Factory. Governor James Isham saw them in the offing, recognized them as interlopers, and prepared to repel them. He loaded his cannon, chopped down the beacons used for navigation, and pulled up the buoys that marked the channel leading up to the post. He then warned the ships not to come any closer unless they were authorized to do so by either the company or the Crown. As it turned out, both captains held commissions as privateers, commissions that required all British subjects to help the bearers in every way possible. Isham had no choice, then, but to offer them whatever assistance they asked for. Apart from such formal obligations, however, he held himself politely aloof. The vessels were wintered in Ten Shillings Creek, five miles above the fort. After burying their beer to keep it from freezing, the men built a two-story house measuring sixteen by twenty feet because the ships themselves were too cold and damp to live in.

The winter was not particularly uncomfortable. Isham provided the men with suitable clothing, but could do nothing for the scurvy that afflicted them. Henry Ellis, one of the chroniclers of the voyage, stated that they suffered from the 'Want of Proper Food, and an inexcusable Indescretion in the Use of spirituous Licqors, rather than the Intenseness of the Cold.' In the spring, they chopped the vessels out of the eight feet of solid ice that kept them captive, then dropped downstream to Five Fathom Hole. They sailed from there on 24 June 1747, heading north for Roes Welcome; five weeks later, they were riding quietly at anchor in Wager Bay. During the next two weeks, the bay was thoroughly and systematically explored by small parties—including both captains—that followed the shore in longboats. The assembled officers held a meeting aboard the *Dobbs* on 14 August, at which they expressed the unanimous opinion that the inlet was a bay rather than a strait. Middleton's position was fully vindicated. There followed some half-hearted discussion of further exploration, but it quickly subsided, for their primary objective had been achieved. There was little else that they could accomplish, because it was already late in the season, many of the men were ill, and there is a possibility that a mutiny was brewing as well. They prudently sailed home.

The mainland stretching north form Churchill had now been explored in considerable detail as far as Repulse Bay and Frozen Strait, with the single exception of Chesterfield Inlet. This inlet, as we have seen, was discovered in 1722 by Scroggs; it had been sighted several times since then, but was not fully explored until 1762. In that year, Willam Christopher from Fort Prince of Wales sailed his sloop, the *Churchill,* through the inlet and into Baker Lake. The desultory search for a passage leading west from Hudson Bay was finally ended. It had lasted for an even one hundred and fifty years, for Thomas Button had discovered that coast while engaged in a similar search in 1612.

The next assault on the Arctic was an overland expedition launched from Fort Prince of Wales. Ever since the founding of the post in 1717, the traders had been intrigued by the fact that the natives knew of a source of copper somewhere far to the northwest. As was noted earlier, James Knight and his party were led to their tragic death on Marble Island in attempting to locate that source in 1719-21. Some fifty years later, in 1769, the Company decided to try once more. This time they chose Samuel Hearne, one of their traders who was also an explorer and cartographer, to carry the search. His first attempt was aborted when his Indian guide deserted him far out on the barren lands; his second attempt ended when he accidently broke his quadrant, and had to return to the fort. He was successful, finally, on his third attempt. He found a disappointingly thin deposit of copper scattered along the banks of a river he named the Coppermine, and then proceeded north to its mouth on Coronation Gulf (See Hearne, 1795), where he arrived on 18 July 1771. He was thus the first European to stand on the arctic coast of North America.

Watching the ice that stretched before him in the still frozen gulf, Hearne knew that he was a long way from home; but even he probably failed to realize how isolated he actually was. To the east, the nearest known point at that time was Cape Dyer, 1300 miles away, on the west side of Davis Strait. Everything in between was blank. To the west, the nearest known point was East Cape, Siberia, and that was 1282 miles away. Fort Churchill itself lay 890 miles to the southeast. It has been estimated that Hearne walked almost 5,000 miles during his explorations of the Northwest Territories.

The next explorer to stand on the arctic coast of Canada was Alexander Mackenzie, a trader and explorer employed by the North West Company (Mackenzie, 1801). He left Fort Chipewyan on Lake Athabaska on 3 June 1789 to explore a mighty river that the Indians said flowed from the western end of Great Slave Lake. Mackenzie had hoped that the river would lead to the Pacific, but it carried him relentlessly north. On 14 July, he was camped on Whale Island in what is now the Mackenzie delta. He realized that he had reached the coast only when he arose next morning to find that his baggage was water, having been swamped by a rising tide. Only then, apparently, did he learn that he had reached the ocean, the Arctic rather that the Pacific (Cooke and Holland, 1978, p. 110). Mackenzie returned to Fort Chipewyan on 12 September, having covered almost 4800 kilometers at an average speed of 47.5 km per day for 101 days.

## Looking Ahead

DURING THE LONG INTERVAL between the first and second acts of our northern drama, other things were happening as well, things that bear directly upon our topic. The most widely known of these events is surely the series of revolutions that shattered the time-honoured patterns of western European behavior. For the first time in its long and turbulent history, a new contestant entered the political arena when thirteen American colonies of Britain decided they would rule themselves. No longer was the political arena reserved for the kings, emperors, dukes, cardinals and popes who had traditionally been the sole contenders for political supremacy. That men might rule themselves was a heady idea—not new, certainly, but still heady—and one that streaked across the political skies like a rocket. It blazed with such intensity that long-dormant seeds of unrest sprouted all over Europe, and in the new world from Mexico to the tip of South America. The American uprising inaugerated what came to be known as the Age of Revolution. So clear was the vision, and so persuasive was the rhetoric of men such as Thomas Paine and Voltaire, that the fires smouldered well into the 1850s.

Long before the age of political revolutions, however, Europe had been subjected to an intellectual revolution that was even more fundamental. For the faith that had provided medieval Europe with its ultimate sanctions and explanations was finally being challenged. When Descartes, a contemporary of Bacon and Galileo, published his *Discourse of Method* in 1637, he laid the foundations of modern philosophy, a system that rejected theology, and exposed all arguments to the cold, impersonal light of reason. For as Bacon had pointed out in his *Novum Organum,* first published in 1620, the deductive processes of medieval theologians and philosophers limited their enquiries to conclusions that were already contained in their premises. The system was closed in that it had no way of dealing with new data, with the results of empirical observations or research. Knowledge, that is, had been derived from the study of authorities. Human understanding of God, and the nature of the Godhead itself, had been derived from the Bible and the commentaries of the early church fathers. Human understanding of God, and of nature—the world that God had created—had been derived from Aristotle.

The scientific revolution that climaxed in the seventeenth century was led by repudiators of all authority, and turned to the world itself for explanations. They counted, weighed, measured and dissected, then formulated hypotheses such as that of Isaac Newton. The effects of the scientific revolution were summarized as follows by a British historian:

Since that revolution overturned the

authority in science not only of the middle ages but of the ancient world—since it ended not only in the eclipse of scholastic philosophy but in the destruction of Aristotelian physics—it outshines everything since the rise of Christianity and reduces the Renaissance and Reformation to the rank of mere episodes, mere internal displacements, within the system of medieval Christendom (Butterfield, 1949, VIII).

It is sometimes difficult for us to realize that change, as we know and experience it today, is a very modern phenomenon. We have become accustomed to grappling with new ideas such as the germ theory in medicine or plate tectonics in geology. We are even more accustomed to accepting new commodities that appear in the marketplace with mechanical regularity—such things as new models in cars, clothing and morals. Although we are not always comfortable with the kinds of changes that occur, we somehow manage to accept them as natural and necessary. For example, the obsolence that we build into our consumer goods is justified on the grounds that it creates employment, which it does, of course. It is equally true that arson and prostitution also create employment, but we never suggest that jobs are created by expanding such activities. The point is that the changes swirling around us today result largely from the seventeenth century is science. Before that intellectual upheaval, the world was seen as essentially static. Both the social and the geographical horizons were stable and enduring. Any changes that did occur—a bit of rape and pillage here, a miracle or two there—were seen merely as ripples on a sea of tranquility.

It was the geographical discoveries of the Portuguese and Spanish that first shattered the medieval illusion of permanence and stability. Because it happened so long ago, we who hark back to that period find it difficult to realize just how suddenly and dramatically the world seemed to be expanding at the time. For each year new coastlines were being added to the map of the world, as were a seemingly endless assortment of islands and continents. And it all happened with amazing speed. The impact of the new geographical discoveries was such that Europeans suddenly found themselves in a world that had actually doubled in size. George Best, the principal chronicler of the Frobisher voyages, commented on this sudden expansion during his discussion of the 1576 expedition: 'Thus it has come to pass,' he said, 'that within the memory of man—within these four score years---more new countries and regions have been discovered than in the previous five thousand' (Kenyon, 1975, p. 22). The navigators and merchants who drove their ships across uncharted oceans changed the very nature of the world with their discoveries. And the ensuing revolution in science changed the nature of humanity itself; it altered the structure of the human mind, the way in which it processed information, to use the currently fashionable phrase. For uncounted centuries, it had been said of the wind that it 'bloweth as it listeth.' On this side of the scientific revolution, however, it simply obeys the laws of physics, as it always did, of course. It was not the wind that had changed, but the way in which people looked at the wind.

It was a different England, then, that sent the second wave of explorers into the Arctic, an England caught up in a scientific and industrial revolution that was reshaping the entire world. These explorers were a new breed; they were naval officers, but they were leading scientific expeditions. They laid down highly accurate maps of the areas they had explored, a skill they learned from Captain James Cook; they described the native people they encountered, and collected specimens of the flora, fauna and geology of the places they visited; they measured the direction and speed of ocean currents, and the temperature and salinity of the sea water; they recorded the variation of the compass, and the strength of the earth's magnetic field. And those parties that wintered in the Arctic carried out astronomical observations as well.

At the end of each expedition, the leader would submit a written report to the Admiralty. These were detailed journals that described the day-by-day activities of the entire party, as recorded in the ship's log. Scientific data were sometimes submitted in appendices to the journal, and sometimes in separate volumes. Because the history of arctic exploration is contained in a superb series of such volumes, a comment on their style might not by out of place. Education at the time was structured around a study of the classics. This resulted in a prose style that was lucid, but extremely formal. The spontaneity of the Elizabethans had disappeared, to be replaced in the nineteenth century journals by an impersonal prose that was clearly derived from the Latin. Its sentences marched across the page with the regular, measured tread of a Roman legion.

The result, in my opinion, is quite depressing. This probably reflects nothing more than a personal preference for Elizabethan prose. But it does make the task of the historian more difficult. For it deprives us of those rich, meaty quotations that can enliven a discussion of the earlier explorers. And furthermore, a prolonged immersion in the self-consciously formal prose of the nineteenth century journals tends to infect the prose style of the historian's own writing.

By the time Britain launched her second attack on the Arctic, she was the undisputed naval power of Europe, and was equally powerful ashore. At the battle of Trafalgar she had demonstrated her naval supremacy; and at the battle of Waterloo she had defeated the massed armies of Europe, and sent their leader into brooding exile on St. Helena. She was flushed with the arrogance of victory, and eager to test her strength against another worthy adversary. That she chose to direct her energies to arctic exploration might be explained by her history. It was the merchants of that same realm, after all, who had started northern exploration. The Muscovy Company had opened a flourishing maritime trade with Russia in 1553; other English merchants had played a leading part in the development of the whale fishery at Spitzbergen. The memory of Sir Francis Drake, John Hawkins, Martin Frobisher, John Cabot, Sir Walter Raleigh and a seemingly endless list of similar figures was still vivid, and their names still reverberated throughout the land. These circumstances alone explain England's interest in a continuing demonstration of her powers. But why the Arctic? There were other fields of endeavour that would have provided an equally acceptable arena and might have turned a tidy profit as well. The answer is probably political rivalry with Russia. John Barrow, Secretary of the Navy at the end of the Napoleonic wars, published a circumpolar map in 1818, a map that graphically compared the northern coastlines of Russia and British North America. The Russian achievements in arctic exploration were set down in a long, sinuous line that stretched from the White Sea to Bering Strait, with only one minor break. The line extended through 150 of longitude, or at 60°30' north, through more than 3,500 miles.

From Cape Prince of Wales on Bering Strait to Cape Dyer on Davis Strait is only 100°43' of longitude, or 2,400 miles. That is, the coast of arctic Russia from the White Sea to Bering Strait was about half again as long as the arctic coast of North America; and the Siberian coastline had been almost completely charted by 1818, when Barrow published his map. The broad stretches of the North American Arctic, on the other hand, were known at only two widely separated points, at the mouth of the Coppermine River, and at the mouth of the Mackenzie River. It was this contrast between the arctic achievements of the Russians and the British that the latter found intolerable. It must have been particularly galling to John Barrow, who directed the activities of the largest navy the world had ever seen, and who had also founded the Royal Geographical Society. In launching a two-pronged attack on the Arctic the same year his map was published, in 1818, Barrow made the opening move in a new assault on the Arctic. The second phase of our north exploration had started.

WHAT REMAINED TO BE SEEN WAS WHETHER the naval authorities in Britain would choose to ignore the portents that were so amply provided by their own history, or would the experiences of such arctic argonauts as Frobisher, Gilbert, Hudson, Button and James be taken into account? Would the authorities choose, rather, to put their faith in what a later age was to laud as the thin red line of empire. By looking upon the Arctic as just one more adversary that would fall before the power and determination that had already made Britain the undisputed ruler of the high seas, Barrow and his associates gave a clear indication of their resolve. The fact that the arctic seas were largely frozen was of no consequence whatever; frozen oceans were still oceans, and would therefore yield to the authority of the British navy.

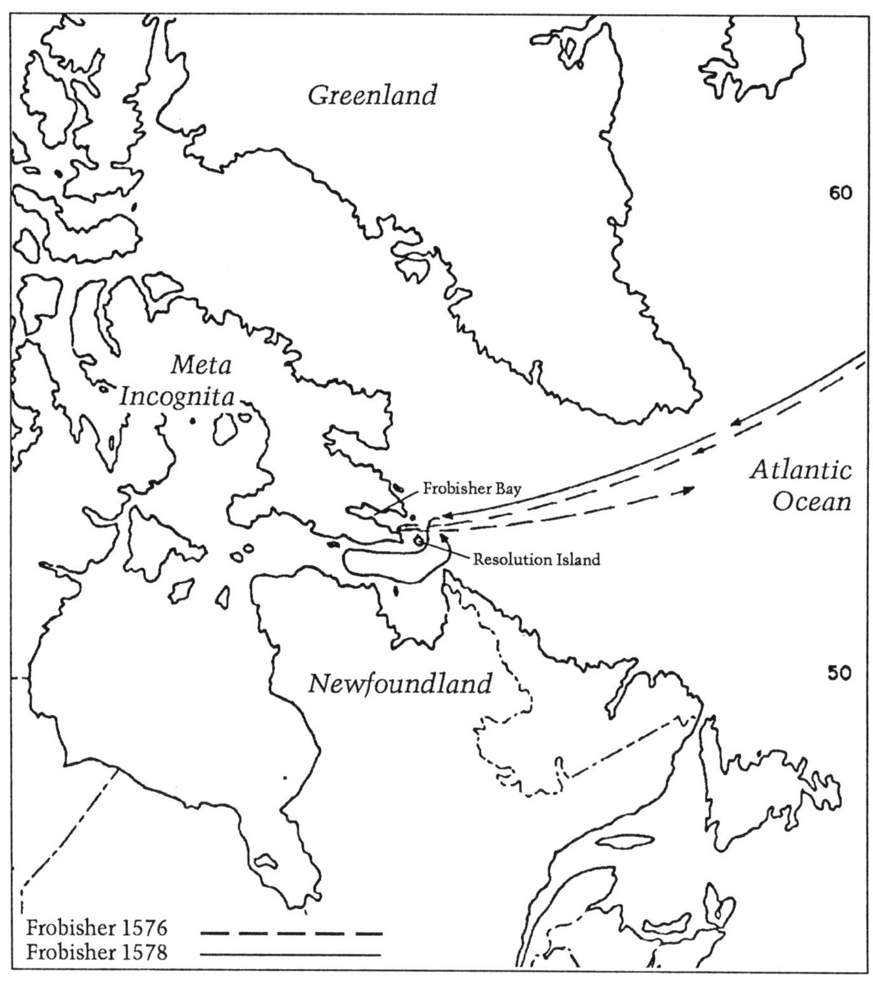
Greenland
60
Meta
Incognita
Frobisher Bay
Atlantic
Ocean
Resolution Island
Newfoundland
50
Frobisher 1576
Frobisher 1578

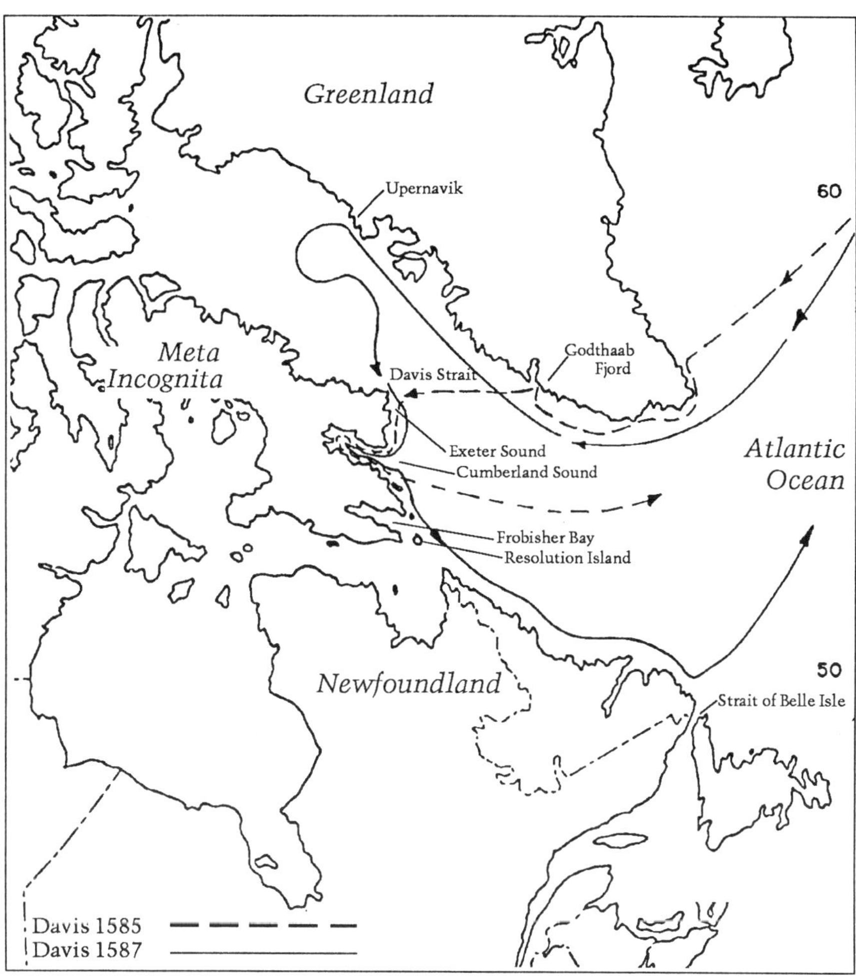
Greenland
Upernavik
60
Meta
Incognita
Davis Strait
Godthaab
Fjord
Exeter Sound
Cumberland Sound
Atlantic
Ocean
Frobisher Bay
Resolution Island
50
Newfoundland
Strait of Belle Isle
Davis 1585
Davis 1587

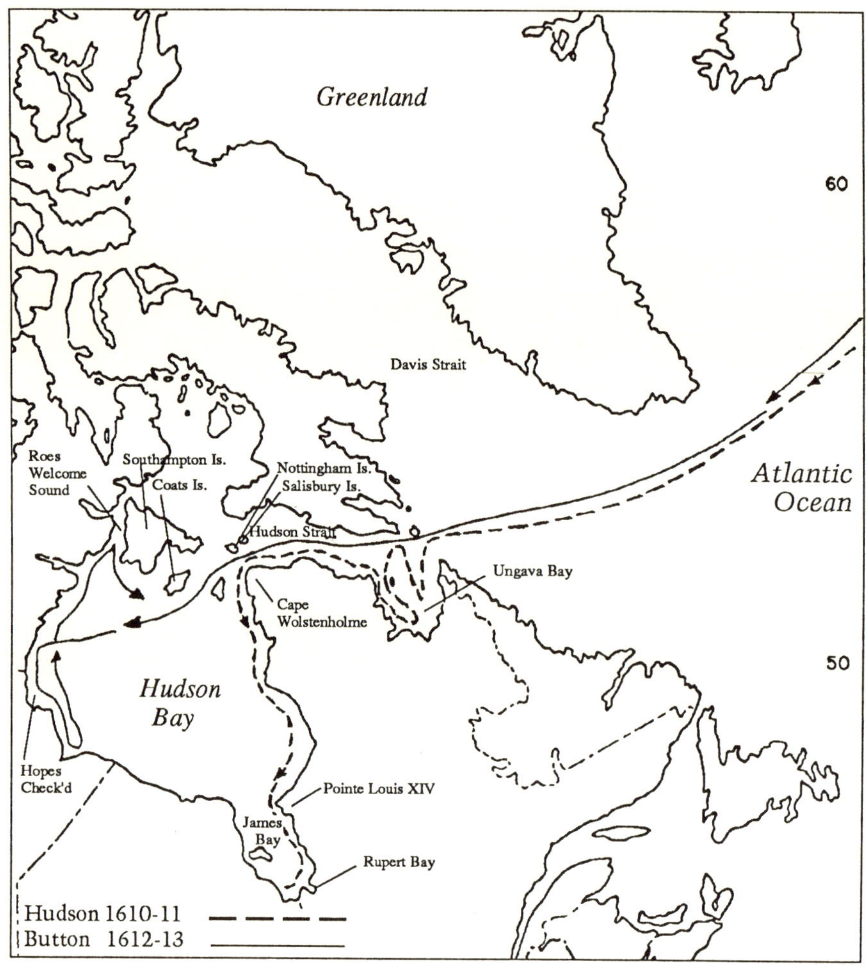
Greenland
60
Davis Strait
Roes
Welcome
Sound
Southampton Is.
Coats Is.
Nottingham Is.
Salisbury Is.
Hudson Strait
Atlantic
Ocean
Ungava Bay
Cape
Wolstenholme
50
Hudson
Bay
Hopes
Check'd
Pointe Louis XIV
James
Bay
Rupert Bay
Hudson 1610-11
Button 1612-13

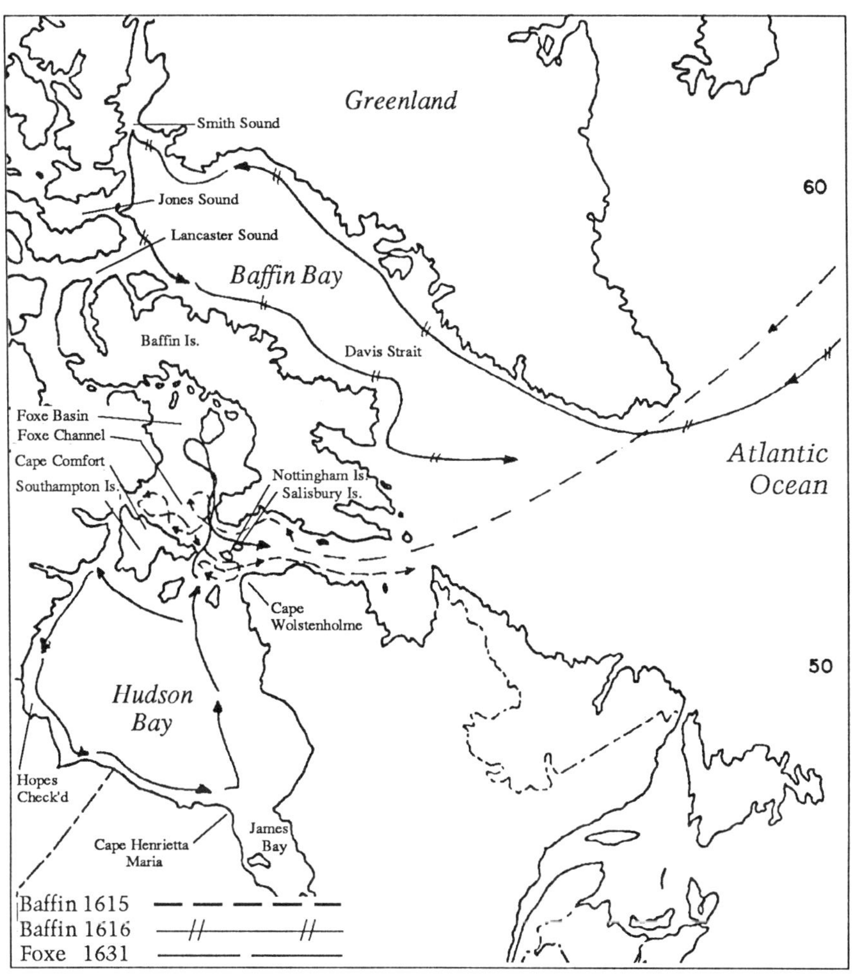
Greenland
Smith Sound
Jones Sound
Lancaster Sound
Baffin Bay
Baffin Is.
Davis Strait
60
Atlantic
Ocean
Foxe Basin
Foxe Channel
Cape Comfort
Southampton Is.
Nottingham Is.
Salisbury Is.
Cape
Wolstenholme
50
Hudson
Bay
Hopes
Check'd
Cape Henrietta
Maria
James
Bay
Baffin 1615
Baffin 1616
Foxe 1631

## Works Cited

ASHER, G. M. (1860). *Henry Hudson the navigator.* London: Hakluyt Society, First Series, No. 27.

BARROW, John. (1818). *A chronological history of voyages into the Arctic regions; undertaken chiefly for the purpose of discovering a North-east, North-west, or polar passage between the Atlantic and Pacific: from the earliest periods of Scandinavian navigation, to the departure of the recent expeditions, under the orders of Captains Ross and Buchan.* London: John Murray.

BEAGLEHOLE, John C. (1974). *The Life of captain James Cook.* Stanford: Stanford University Press.

CHRISTY, Miller. (1894). *The Voyages of captain Luke Foxe of Hull, and captain Thomas James of Bristol, in search of a North-West Passage, in 1631-32 ... 2 vols.* London: Hakluyt Society, First Series, Nos. 88-89.

COLLINSON, Richard. (1867). In George Best (Ed.), *The three voyages of Martin Frobisher, in search of a passage to Cathaia and India by the North-West, A.D. 1576-78, reprinted from the first edition of Hakluyt's voyages, with selections from manuscript documents in the British Museum and State Paper Office.* London: Hakluyt Society.

COOK, James. (1784). *A Voyage to the Pacific Ocean.* Dublin: Printed for H. Chamberlain.

COOKE, Alan & Holland, Clive. (1978). *The Exploration of Northern Canada, 500-1920: a chronology.* Toronto: Arctic History Press.

GILBERT, Humphrey. (1576). *A discourse of a discoverie.*

GOSCH, C. G. A. (1897). *Danish Arctic Expeditions, 1605 to 1620.* London: Hakluyt Society, First Series, No. 97).

HEARNE, Samuel. (1795). *A journey from Prince of Wale's fort, in Hudson's Bay, to the northern ocean undertaken by order of the Hudson's Bay Company, for the discovery of copper mines, a North West Passage, etc. in the years 1769, 1770, 1771 & 1772*. London: A Strahan and T. Cadell.

KENYON, Walter. (1975-1). *The Strange and Dangerous Voyage of Captain Thomas James*. Toronto: Royal Ontario Museum.

KENYON, Walter. (1975-2). *Tokens of Possession: the Northern Voyages of Martin Frobisher*. Toronto: Royal Ontario Museum.

KENYON, Walter. (1980). *The Journals of Jens Munk, 1619-1620*. Toronto: Royal Ontario Museum.

LUBBOCK, Basil. (1968). *The Arctic Whalers*. Glasgow: Brown.

MACKENZIE, Alexander. (1801). *Voyages from Montreal, on the St. Lawrence, through the Continent of North America, to the frozen and Pacific Oceans, in the years 1789-1793*. London: Cadell.

MARKHAM, Albert Hastings. (1880). *The voyages and works of John Davis the navigator*. London: Hakluyt Society, First Series, No. 59.

MARKHAM, Clements Robert. (1881). *The Voyages of William Baffin, 1612-1622*. London: Hakluyt Society, First Series, No. 63.

ROSS, John. (1819). *A voyage of discovery, made under the orders of the Admiralty, in His Majesty's Ships Isabella and Alexander, for the purpose of exploring Baffin's Bay, and inquiring into the probability of a North-west Passage*. London: John Murray.

RUNDALL, Thomas. (1849). *Narratives of voyages towards the North-west, in search of a passage to Cathay and India. 1496 to 1631. With selections from the early records of the Honourable the East India Company and from mss. in the British Museum*. London: Hakluyt Society, First Series, No. 5).

SMITH, John. (1627). *A sea grammar.* Amsterdam: Da Capo Press.

Stevens, Henry. (1886). *The dawn of British trade in the East Indies as recorded in the minutes of the East India Company, 1599-1603, containing an account of the formation of the company, the first adventure and Weymouth's voyage in search of the North-West Passage.* London.

TAYLOR, E. G. R. (1959). *The troublesome voyage of Captain Edward Fenton, 1582-1583: narratives & documents.* Cambridge: Hakluyt Society at the University Press.

WOODALL, John. (1617). *The surgeons mate.* London: Printed by E. Griffin for L. Lisle.